Thinking Through Education

Thinking Through Ethics and Values in Primary Education

THE UNIVERSITY OF
WINCHESTER

Thinking Through Education

Thinking Through Ethics and Values in Primary Education

Editors: Gianna Knowles and Vini Lander

Los Angeles | London | New Delhi
Singapore | Washington DC

Learning Matters
An imprint of SAGE Publications Ltd
1 Oliver's Yard
55 City Road
London EC1Y 1SP

SAGE Publications Inc.
2455 Teller Road
Thousand Oaks, California 91320

SAGE Publications India Pvt Ltd
B 1/I 1 Mohan Cooperative Industrial Area
Mathura Road
New Delhi 110 044

SAGE Publications Asia-Pacific Pte Ltd
3 Church Street
#10-04 Samsung Hub
Singapore 049483

Editor: Amy Thornton
Development Editor: Clare Weaver
Production Controller: Chris Marke
Project Management: Deer Park Productions, Tavistock
Marketing Manager: Catherine Slinn
Cover Design: Toucan Design
Typeset by: Pantek Media, Maidstone, Kent
Printed by: TJ International Ltd, Padstow, Cornwall

Library of Congress Control Number: 2012933568

British Library Cataloguing in Publication Data

A catalogue record for this book is available from the British Library

ISBN: 978 0 85725 857 1
ISBN: 978 0 85725 733 8 (pbk)

MIX
Paper from
responsible sources
FSC
www.fsc.org   FSC® C013056

Contents

About the authors

Linda Cooper is a lecturer in Education Studies at the University of Chichester. She has worked in education for 16 years, both as a primary school teacher and as a lecturer. Before commencing her post at Chichester, Linda also worked at Portsmouth University as a lecturer in Early Childhood Studies and at Bishop Grosseteste University College, Lincoln with the Initial Teacher Training team. She has a range of interests and has published in the field of technology, physical development and the humanities.

Sally Hawkins is a senior lecturer in Education Studies at the University of Chichester, where she co-ordinates the Professional Studies input for undergraduate and postgraduate students on initial teacher training programmes. Prior to this, she worked in a range of Hampshire primary schools for 17 years. She has led and managed many staff teams and has provided curriculum in-service training and support material for schools and HE providers in the South of England. She has a keen interest in creativity and the many aspects of child development.

Carol Hughes is a lecturer in Education Studies at the University of Chichester. Carol is a former deputy-headteacher, with over 25 years' teaching experience. She has taught in mainstream secondary, middle and primary schools in a variety of settings throughout England. Before joining the University of Chichester in 2009, Carol worked on a part-time basis for the University of Sussex as an assessor on their primary graduate teacher programme. Her specialist curriculum area is mathematics and the focus for her MA research was girls' under-achievement in mathematics.

Gianna Knowles is a lecturer in Education Studies at the University of Chichester. She has also worked with teacher trainee students from across Europe at the University of Jönköping in Sweden. Gianna has over 12 years' experience of teaching in primary schools in England, in London and the Midlands. She has worked in Local Authority Advisory services, working with individual teachers and whole-schools' staffs to develop school-wide practice and policy. Gianna has experience of being an OfSTED inspector and a reviewer for the Quality Assurance Agency. Her research interest is in the area of social justice, inclusion and diversity. She has written widely about education and learning, particularly in the area of how children from diverse families and backgrounds, or who have a disability or SEN, can best be enabled to achieve in their learning.

Vini Lander is the Head of Primary Programmes at the University of Chichester. She was also Deputy Director of Multiverse for five years. This was a TDA-funded professional resource network on achievement and diversity. As part of her role in Multiverse, Vini has delivered training sessions across England to student teachers and teacher educators on diversity, inclusion and achievement. Vini has also delivered lectures to teachers and teacher educators in Berlin, Hamburg and Munich.

Vini worked in mainstream schools teaching science and A level biology for a number of years. She also worked in a specialist role with pupils having English as an Additional Language. At the University of Chichester Vini teaches on the primary undergraduate, postgraduate and Master's level programmes. Vini's research interests lie in the field of race, ethnicity and diversity, particularly with reference to initial teacher education. She has completed her doctoral research in this area.

Glenn Stone is currently a senior lecturer in Education at the University of Chichester. His research interests include the impact of ICT on the teaching of English and teaching through the use of learning platforms. Glenn has published a number of articles in this field. Glenn is currently engaged in research regarding aspects of teacher identity both within schools and through Initial Teacher Training. Prior to working at the university, Glenn was a mainstream primary school teacher and then a member of the Senior Leadership Team for a large junior school.

Barbara Thompson is currently a principal lecturer and subject leader for the MA in Education at the University of Chichester, having previously led Chichester's PGCE (Postgraduate Certificate in Education) Primary Programme. Before moving into higher education she spent 17 years in primary schools in the Midlands and the North of England. Barbara's area of research is gender issues and, before working at Chichester, she was an Open University tutor for the MA module in Gender and Education. Barbara has a PhD in Gender, Management and Leadership and a number of publications in this field.

Introduction
Gianna Knowles

This book is designed to enable the reader to reflect on, and to articulate, what they believe education to be about and how they believe educating children should be approached. That those involved in education can reflect on and articulate their beliefs about education is important for two reasons. Firstly, as part of the application and interview process for a post in an educational setting, applicants are expected to be able to discuss the values and ethics that underpin the professional skills, knowledge and understanding they possess. Indeed, the Department for Education states that: *appropriate self-evaluation, reflection and professional development activity is critical to improving teachers' practice at all career stages* (DfE, 2011c, p.3). Therefore, both the government and an educational setting, such as a school, want to be assured that those being employed to educate children have given considerable thought to what they believe education to be about and the principles that underpin how they go about educating the children in their care. In particular a school will want to know these things about an applicant at this and the interview stage as they need to make a judgement about whether the applicant will support the values and ethics that the school believes to be important. Therefore, whether you have yet to apply for your first post in a school or are undertaking professional development to improve your practice, it is important to have a clear idea about what you believe is important about education and educating children. The second reason for this book is that education and educational policy can seem to be in a constant state of flux. For those working in education, having considered and reflected on personal beliefs about the core values of education and particular educational practices will provide a strong platform from which to purposefully respond to new demands and initiatives as they arise.

In terms of recent changes in educational policy the Education Act 2011 brings with it the need for schools to consider and possibly review various aspects of their provision: for example, how they approach discipline and behaviour management. Schools, particularly through Free Schools and Academies, have the possibility of more autonomy, bringing with it more freedom to decide how they construct and deliver the education they offer their communities. The National Curriculum has been reviewed, as has provision for children who are disabled or who have special educational needs (SEN); again, these changes require schools to revisit their provision in these areas. The government has also reviewed the standards teachers must achieve in their training and continue to maintain throughout their teaching career. In the current document that outlines the standards for teachers the government states that teachers have a duty to *uphold public trust in the profession and maintain high standards of ethics and behaviour* (DfE, 2011c, p.8). Further to this, those educating children must show: *tolerance of and respect for the rights of others* (p.8); this includes: *not undermining fundamental British values, including democracy, the rule of law, individual liberty and mutual respect, and tolerance of those with different faiths and beliefs* (p.8). While there have been changes in these aspects of education, the government also seeks constantly to remind schools that, however they go about educating their children, part of their core purpose is to seek to maintain: *a rigorous focus on . . . high standards . . . a determination to narrow attainment gaps between pupils from different parts of society . . . and a rigorous and stretching curriculum* (DfE, 2010, p.8).

From the above we can see that ethics and values are regarded as an important aspect of education, but we are not necessarily any clearer about what the terms 'ethics' and 'values' might mean. As a general rule, explorations of the notion of ethics discuss the rules we live by, that is, what we rely on as the underpinning principles that guide us in our understanding of what is right and wrong, or correct and incorrect. The notion of value is about those things we believe to be important to us and feel are valuable for wider society too. The government gives a good starting point in thinking through what values might mean by signalling that *democracy, the rule of law, individual liberty and mutual respect and tolerance of different faiths and beliefs* (DfE, 2011c, p.8) are concepts to be thought of being of considerable value in UK society. Of course, democracy, liberty, tolerance, respect for others and for the law of the land are not values special to the UK, or even to particular religious, ethnic or cultural groups that form part of the diverse nature of UK society. Many peoples across the world hold these concepts to be of value and all these values are considered as being universal fundamental human rights. That this is so can be seen in the preamble to the United Nation's Universal Declaration of Human Rights, which begins by affirming that: *the foundation of freedom, justice and peace in the world* is that these values are of importance for all people as they are about *the inherent dignity and the equal and inalienable rights of all members of the human family* (United Nations, 1948).

What is considered as being of value in a society can more often be agreed on than the ethics that determine how values are upheld and expressed. Simply put, ethics are those rules we use to guide us in knowing what correct or incorrect behaviour is, in this instance with regard to those things we see as being of value. Therefore, while many will agree liberty to be of value, different individuals, social, cultural, religious and ethnic groups may interpret behaviours linked to the expression of liberty in many seemingly different ways. For example, some believe liberty is about absolute freedoms to do whatever the individual may want to do, while others would say liberty is about the exercise of personal wishes up to the point where they affect the liberty of others. Still others will say some people are too young, too unwell or because of their behaviour cannot be allowed to have as much liberty as others, while some will be seen as misusing their liberty through coercing or persuading others to behaviours that infringe liberties – for example, by encouraging lack of tolerance, rioting or conforming to certain sets of rules.

Very quickly then, we can see that the challenge of exploring ethics and values in a diverse society such as the UK is that there seem to be so many differences between individuals, groups and communities in terms of what is regarded as accepted behaviour. Similarly, there will be variation in some of the values held by different individuals, groups and communities. Therefore, when in the classroom, it can sometimes be hard to know what rules for behaviours to expect from children and to encourage them to adopt. While at the same time it can also be hard to juggle tensions between knowing what aspects of learning should be prioritised over others, because some areas of learning are seen as being more valuable than others. For example, is teaching children social skills more, or less, valuable than teaching them mathematics? It can also be tempting when discussing concepts such as ethics and values to think they are ideas relating only high-flown abstruse philosophical thinking about particularly difficult issues. The reality, however, as we have already touched on, is that ethics and values are about the sorts of day-to-day, minute-by-minute decisions we make about what to do in the classroom throughout the school day.

A further challenge in discussing ethics and values is that while this book can raise questions with the reader about what is of value in education and what ethical approaches should be taken to educating children, what it cannot do is provide a straightforward answer to all questions discussed – in part because there is no straightforward answer. What this book can do, however, is work with you, the reader, to further explore the complexity of ethics and values as they relate to primary education and to help you analyse and articulate your own ethics and values in relation to primary education, providing you with the confidence to be able to state your own approaches to the issues discussed. To do this, the book will begin with a more in-depth exploration of the notion of ethics and values and how individuals, groups and communities have developed ethical principles that become the foundations that guide behaviour. It will explore how rules vary between generations and different groups and communities, discussing how, usually, the ethics used by individuals and groups are linked to social, cultural and religious influences that may be part of that group's identity, both historically and in current practice. The book will explore how our own ethical principles may be influenced by dominant historical ethical discourses in the social, cultural and religious communities we belong to and how thinking in these areas has been shaped by the wider historical and cultural development of the UK as a whole. Having explored with the reader the wider notion of ethics and values in this way, and worked with the reader to help them understanding their own values and ethics, the book then explores ethics and values in relation to different aspects of education in the primary school phase.

What we value about education and the ethics of how we should go about educating children are issues that have concerned individuals and societies for centuries. For example, the Greek philosopher Plato, born 427 BCE, discussed how, in terms of education: *it is considered intrinsically valuable to be knowledgeable, and many pursue education for this reason alone* (Purshouse, 2010, p.29). That is to say, education and learning has a value of itself. It is of value to be educated and to know something, rather than to know nothing. Knowledge also has an instrumental value, however, in that as a consequence of having knowledge we can access other things that are seen as having value, including how *knowledge might also help, for instance, when it comes to pursuing a career* (2010, p.29). More recently, it is R.S. Peters who has been most influential in exploring ethics and values in education in Britain. Although first published in 1966,

Peters' *Ethics and education* (1970) has had a lasting impact on the way the notion of education is discussed in the UK. In his book Peters invites us, just as Plato did over 2000 years ago, to consider what it is we value about education and value to such an extent that we, as a society, invest so much of our time, thought, energy and money in ensuring that children have the *right* education and a *good* education.

In exploring this first point, Peters suggests that the term 'education' has no one meaning. In fact, we use the term to cover a range of ideas and practices which we, by usage of the term and familiarity with what in the UK is deemed education, come to have a general understanding of what education might be. Our personal, general understanding will have much overlap with others' understanding of the term, but there may also be some difference in the way the term is used by different individuals or groups. Peters describes this way of using the term 'education' as its having *central* and *peripheral usages* (Peters, 1970, p.24). That is, the term seems to have something central, or core to it which is specific to education and makes it distinctive by comparison with other concepts, like the concept of justice, for example. We can recognise something as being part of this central idea because it is about that which is relevant to education, learning and teaching, for example. However, how we then agree collectively on the more peripheral or wider aspects of education and what is of value in this peripheral area is a different matter. For example, we may agree education is about learning, but not about what learning is or how ethically it is best enabled to happen. Often our disagreements arise because of what we see as the value of different aspects of education and the way in which we want these values to be upheld in educational practice – that is, our ethical approach to putting into practice what we value in education. I might, for example, value as being educational the learning of times (or multiplication) tables ($1 \times 2 = 2$, $2 \times 2 = 4$, etc.) and I might believe the ethically correct way of doing this is by memorising tables by rote. The colleagues I work with and the children I teach may value and believe something very different with respect to this aspect of mathematics and go about the learning in a different way, yet still agree learning about multiplication and understanding something about the use of numbers in this way is an important part of mathematics education.

It is the sorts of questions and issues about education discussed above, which as yet have no clearly agreed-on answers, although we know in the West that they were raised 2000 years ago by philosophers such as Plato, that we continue to concern ourselves with in this book. We are still concerned with these issues because our role in school requires that we be part of decisions that need to be made about school policy. In all schools decisions about what should be taught, when and how and why, what particular teaching methods should be used, how and what children should be taught about right and wrong, how and when children should be disciplined, and what values the school feels are important to develop as part of school's vision and ethos all need to be made. Indeed, you will probably be asked some questions at interview that will require you to give an indication of your thinking about such issues, otherwise how will those thinking of offering you the job know if you are going to enjoy working at the school and if, indeed, you are the kind of person they will want to work with?

As we have seen, discussions about ethics and values can be complex, particularly when they can seem areas of enquiry that have no straightforward answers. Therefore, to help you in your thinking about the issues and themes raised in the book, each chapter contains a case study and a number of critical thinking exercises. The case studies help illustrate the points being discussed and the critical thinking exercises will help you to examine your own thoughts and beliefs about the issues. In this way, you will be able to develop sound arguments to explain what you believe to be of value in education and the ethics that underpin how you would go about educating children. While each case study and critical thinking exercise is specific to the idea under discussion, the critical thinking skills needed to explore the concepts are generic. The specific reflective skills developed through the critical thinking exercises are those listed in the table below.

Analyse	Why you think things are happening in the way they are, what might be the reasons that things happen in the way they do?
Articulate	Think through how you might put forward, in discussion, your ideas and your thinking about issues and situations.
Challenge	Sometimes people just assume this is how things should be and act without thinking things through. What are the assumptions people are making in particular situations; do you think they are basing their actions on careful thought; do you think there are other factors that need to be considered that may be being overlooked?
Compare	What are the pros and cons of approaching situations differently? This might be acting differently, thinking differently, in any given situation.
Consider	How might people explain their actions; could things be different?
Discuss	'Unpick' the situation and think though or talk about all the elements that contribute to it.
Experiment	Try approaching things differently – what happens?
Explore	Think about what might be the different consequences and outcomes of the situations you are observing or discussing. Ask yourself: does it have to be like this; are there alternative ways of approaching this situation?
Illustrate	Can you give examples and evidence to support your discussion and ideas?
Imagine	Think about all the different possible approaches to a situation. Put yourself in the position of someone else in the situation – a child for example; how might you see things then?
Motivation	What factors are having an impact on the situation? Are personal factors involved? Are people responding to outside influences? Who stands to gain or lose from the situation?
Observe	What is happening; what do you actually see others doing (which may be different from what they say or think is happening); how are people acting and behaving in particular situations?
Synthesise	How does thinking about a situation in different critical ways help you pull together a range of factors to develop an argument for finding a way forward, or provide you with good reasons for why you do the things you do?

Discussions about ethics and values as they relate to education can be very wide-ranging; the chapter synopsis below gives you a brief outline of the themes covered in this book. Whatever your particular interest with regard to ethics and values in education, it is recommended you begin with reading the first two chapters of the book as these will help to give you the reflective skills and contextual knowledge and understanding to help you better tackle the remaining chapters.

Chapter 1 explores the two main themes central to the book, that is: what are ethics and what do we mean by values? It discusses how ethics are about what human beings believe to be right or wrong, or to be correct or incorrect ways of behaving, while values are about those things we deem to be important. The key ideas discussed in the chapter are the notions of ethics and values, how the central concepts of divine commands, reason, duty, consequences, absolutism, relativism and being of good character have helped shape values, attitudes, behaviours and beliefs in UK society.

Chapter 2 examines how our ethics and values may shape our response to social diversity within education, and the critical thinking exercises in this chapter are designed to challenge thinking and help to identify how ethics and values are used not only to respond to situations but also how they may sometimes be adapted as a result of such a challenge. The chapter explores how many of our values and ethical codes are formed within the family and the wider institutions that we as individuals engage with. Our values are informed and shaped by our experiences through childhood and throughout our life. The context of our family structure, our age, ethnicity, gender, class and sexuality as well as other factors influence the ethics and values we believe in and uphold and, therefore, the values and ethics we bring to our classroom. The key ideas discussed are: cultural values; tolerance versus acceptance; dominant discourse; plurality and uniformity.

Chapter 3 builds on the ideas explored in Chapters 1 and 2 and begins to apply them to specific issues to do with education. Chapters 1 and 2 explore what is meant by values and ethics and how these concepts apply in a diverse society such as the UK. Having acknowledged these challenges in discussing values and ethics in a pluralist society Chapter 3 begins to consider ideas fundamental to our discussion of ethics and values in education. The key ideas discussed are the notion of what education might be about, how we view children and childhood, children's voice and teaching children to behave.

Chapter 4 explores ethics and values that impact on the school curriculum. Whereas the preceding chapters explore the wider concepts the book deals with, this is the first of five chapters that look at these concepts as they apply directly to specific aspects of education, beginning with the curriculum. The key ideas discussed in the chapter are how we decide what a school curriculum should cover, in terms of skills, knowledge and understanding, including whose view of skills knowledge, culture, values and ethics should lead the curriculum. The chapter discusses the idea that the curriculum is always out of date and asks who should be in charge of making decisions about the content of the curriculum – the government, the school, the local community, or the child?

Chapter 5 continues the theme of looking at specific aspects of education, in this instance leadership and management. The chapter asks you to consider how ethics and values relate to management and leadership and to analyse what you understand by these terms. It will explore how ethics and values relate to management and leadership tasks and looks at how managers and leaders might manage differently, depending on their own ethics and values. The chapter will explore the notion that over the past few decades there has been the introduction of what is often called *the marketplace* into education and that this has led to tensions in what values and ethics should underpin the ways in which educational institutions are managed and led. The key ideas discussed are what we mean by leadership and management, ethics and values in leadership and management, the impact of gender on leadership and management, education and the marketplace, recent value shifts in education and leadership, management and being an effective school.

Chapter 6 further develops the notion of what education might be said to be for, or put another way, what the purpose of education is, in particular giving thought to the ethics of how we should go about the process of education. The chapter also discusses how managing children's behaviour and teaching them about how to behave is often regarded as a value of education. For these reasons you are asked to consider what your values with regard to children's behaviour are and the ethics of teaching children both how to behave and what good and bad behaviour might be. The key ideas discussed are: teaching and learning, behaviourism, constructivism and the importance of play, assessing learning, teaching through creativity, the classroom environment and behaviour management.

Chapter 7 discusses as its key themes the relationship between values and ethics as they relate to children and childhood and how those translate into the education we provide for them. That is, the chapter explores how our own view of what we believe children and childhood to be about will impact on the values and ethics we bring to education. For example, we might value education not only for the skills, knowledge and understanding it may teach a child but also because it may have a value in enriching their lives generally. One of the values of education may be what we learn to enable us to function in society and earn a wage, but many believe education has a wider value, that of enabling us to *fulfil our potential* and enable us to achieve overall wellbeing. The key ideas discussed in the chapter are Dewy and the holistic view of education, perceptions of childhood, children's voice, the development of responsible adults, the voice of the child, school councils, circle time, involving children in target-setting and assessment and international comparisons.

Chapter 8, as the final chapter, reflects on how this book has explored what ethics and values are and how they apply to the concepts of diversity, society, the curriculum, school organisation, the classroom and finally, but not least importantly, children. Within each of these chapters and themes you have been invited to consider your own position and ethics in response to these themes. This chapter will again touch on some of the previous themes but will also highlight some other ways in which ethics and values can underpin a teacher's role. It begins by exploring how important ethics and values are when applying for a teaching post. Teachers' status as professionals is then explored and an argument is put forward that in order to maintain this status, teachers must be ethical. The ethics of teachers' accountability is also put under the spotlight in order to help the reader reflect on how this influences teachers and can force them to work through ethical dilemmas. Finally, the possibility of staying true to your ethics and values, becoming virtuous in the process, is put forward as an intrinsic part of long-term teacher success.

The key ideas discussed are personal ethics and values, schools with specific values and ethics, ethical commitment, teacher professionalism, professional integrity, utilitarianism, performance management and virtue ethics.

1

What are ethics and values?

Gianna Knowles

Chapter Focus

The critical thinking exercises in this chapter focus on:

- ⊙ **analysing** what form the underlying principles of the issues being discussed;
- ⊙ **articulating** what underpins your own approach to the issues being discussed;
- ⊙ **challenging** assumptions;
- ⊙ **comparing** a range of approaches and outcomes;
- ⊙ **considering** what ideas provide the most helpful way forward to resolving conflicting situations;
- ⊙ **discussing** the tensions between competing ideas;
- ⊙ **experimenting** with a range of solutions and situations;
- ⊙ **exploring** how issues can be approached in different ways;
- ⊙ **imagining** different solutions to the issues explored;
- ⊙ **observing** how different people deal with different issues;
- ⊙ **synthesising** different ideas to try to reach a way forward.

The key ideas discussed are: **ethics**, **values**, **divine commands**, **reason**, **duty**, **consequences**, **absolutism**, **relativism** and **being of good character**.
This chapter is particularly relevant to Teachers' Standards: **1**, **2**, **7** and **8**.

Introduction

The study of ethics is about the study of what human beings believe to be right or wrong, or to be correct or incorrect ways of behaving. Therefore, ethics can be said to be the rules we use to help us decide what is the right or wrong thing to do in any given situation, or the correct or incorrect action to perform in that situation, while values are about those things we deem to be important. Therefore, if ethics is about knowing how to react or behave in particular circumstances values, in relation to ethics, are about those things we feel it is important to have rules about dealing with.

Key idea: **Ethics and values**

What are ethics and values?

As human beings there are many things we deem to be important to us. Some of these will be personal preferences about what we feel is important – for example, it may be important to us that we never miss a certain programme on television. For whatever reason, that particular programme is of value to us, maybe because it gives us pleasure or educates and informs us.

However, usually there are things that as human beings we feel are of far more value than personal preferences about television programmes. For example, human life itself, family, honesty and living in a just society. When discussing the notion of values, this book is concerned with exploring those values that fall into this second category.

Of course personal views do impact on how we may think about values such as the importance of family, honesty and justice, and this is an issue central to this book. That is, I might know what is of value to me but what do I do in situations where other people have values different from mine – particularly in a school, where we are all supposed to work together for the good of the children and their families?

So, if values are the things that are of importance to us, ethics then are the sets of rules that help us know how to behave correctly in relation to those values. And similarly, we know that just as different people value things in different ways, they will also have different rules that they use to guide their actions in relation to their values. These differences in rules are again something we will explore throughout this book.

CASE STUDY

Anushka was at work when her best friend, Katy, rushed up to her and told her delightedly that she had just 'found' £50 on the floor in the corridor outside. Katy went on to say, 'Wow, I could really do with this money right now – do you think I should keep it?'

This case study illustrates how often we need to draw on our own system of values and ethics. Situations like this happen frequently throughout the day. Something happens that requires us, almost without thinking, to act on concepts that we believe to be of value. In this instance, Anushka needs to think about the value she places on friendship and also the value she places on concepts such as honesty and justice. However, the challenge Anushka faces is how she reconciles the tension between what she values more, friendship or honesty, and how her values impact on what she then decides to do in the situation, that is, what she believes is ethically the right or wrong thing to do. Consider yourself in Anushka's position in this situation. You have probably been brought up with some quite straightforward guidance about what it means to be honest and about what should be done in situations like this. However, because this situation involves someone you are very close to and care about and, because whatever you say will impact on your relationship with this person, not to mention that you are aware of their particular circumstances, you may feel that you are less sure of what you should do.

It can be tempting when discussing concepts like ethics and values to think they are ideas relating only to high-flown abstruse philosophical thinking about particularly difficult issues. However, the reality is, ethics and values are about the sorts of day-to-day, minute-by-minute decisions we make about what to do in cases such as the one we are currently discussing. If a complete stranger had told us they had found the £50 we would probably give advice about where to take it so it could be claimed by its owner. But when our friend tells us they have found the money, it may be harder to give the same advice.

In day-to-day life, it may not matter that we are flexible in how we use our rules to guide our actions, depending on whom we are dealing with. But, in our role in school it may be that we have to consider not only what we are going to do in a particular situation, but how, through what we do decide to do, we are modelling to children what they too should do in similar situations. Consider this: you are working with a group of children when your hard-up friend comes up to you and says, delightedly 'I've just found £50 outside in the corridor.' The children look at you to see what you are going to do.

Key idea: **Differences**

How do we reconcile tensions between different approaches to ethics and values?

Although we have only just begun to explore the notion of ethics and values and how they relate to primary education, we have, very quickly, run into more questions than we seem to have answered. For example, it seems:

- there can be a variety of rules – or ethics – about what we should or should not do in particular situations;
- that even our own set of rules may differ depending on the situations we find ourselves in;
- that whatever our ethics and values, our role in school may require us to model particular ethics and values in ways that we had not previously considered;
- our role in a school may require us to consider our ethics and values alongside those of the wider school community and mean we need to be able to deal with situations where our ethics and values might be at odds with the ethics and values of others in that community.

As we begin to explore these issues, it is worth bearing in mind, as Campbell (2003) states: *the point of ethics is not to moralise or to dictate what is to be done* (2003, p.9), but rather it is about finding some *tools for thinking about difficult matters, recognizing from the start – as the very rationale for ethics, in fact – that the world is seldom so simple or clear-cut* (p.9).

Further thinking about what ethics mean

Critical thinking exercise 1

Consider the following comment:

> *"While teachers as professionals may agree on the objective principles of fairness and honesty, for example, they may, within the context of their own individual schools and classrooms, interpret them differently in the course of their daily practice."* (Campbell, 2003, p.19)

1 **Consider** what Campbell means by *principles of fairness and honesty*.

2. Do you agree with Campbell, or **challenge** her assumption that individual teachers may interpret fairness and honesty differently?

3. **Imagine** you are a child in a school where different teachers have different interpretations of fairness and honesty. What might be the impact on you as a child?

Comment

At the beginning of the chapter it was suggested that when we are discussing ethics we are concerned about the rules we use to guide us in knowing how to act in ways that are correct in particular situations. One of the interesting things about ethics is that behaviour is very public. That is, it is possible to know something about a person through the way they behave and, therefore, to be able to gain some understanding about their ethics, the rules they live their life by, since e*thical standards are inherently public; they define what we do to, for, and with one another* (Campbell, 2003, p.16). So while you may have been thinking you have no particular set of rules that you live by, as soon as you act in response to an ethical situation it is very clear to those around what your rules are. Let us go back to the issues of the 'found £50'. What would the way you thought about dealing with the situation say to others about the ethics you live your life by?

Key idea: **Values**

How do we know what should be of value?

For us to know how to behave in particular situations we need to have some understanding of the importance we, as individuals, and possibly as a society, attach to the different aspects of a given situation. If we once again return to our 'found £50' situation, we can see that the situation only merits discussion and an examination of what is right and wrong, or ethical, in the situation because the situation contains within it a requirement to act and a range of possible actions that we could take. Some would be the correct way to act and other actions would be viewed as being incorrect. Similarly, that we need to consider different ways of acting in the situation shows that, in this instance, we attach value to the notions of honesty, justice, friendship and fairness. Otherwise, if we did not value these concepts we would not be anxious about doing the correct thing in the situation and seeking both to help our friend and ensure we do so in ways that do not damage the notion of honesty and justice.

Critical thinking exercise 2

In the previous critical thinking exercise you were asked to consider the concepts of *fairness and honesty*. These are abstract concepts, that is, they do not exist in the same concrete way as a chair or a table can be said to exist. You cannot touch fairness, but you can see it happening in practice – or where it is absent from a situation. Therefore, while we can give an actual monetary value to a concrete object, such as a chair, we cannot give a value in terms of money to something like fairness. But this does not detract from the fact we find it has value. We do seem to feel that fairness is something we would not want to lose or have damaged, because it has a value to us and to society, a value other than that which can be represented in purely financial terms.

1. **Consider** what abstract values form part of our thinking about the case of the 'found £50'.

2. **Analyse** why you believe society might regard these concepts as having value. For example, what would we, as a society, lose if we did not value these concepts and protect them through our actions?

3. **Experiment** with thinking about how society protects and behaves with regard to these values and what might society be like if we did not have some values we held in common and all thought were important. For example, what if you behaved in a way that was fair, but others did not?

Comment

What we are using to guide us in deciding where the right and wrong is in this situation is the value we give to some of the abstract concepts implicit in the situation. That is to say, however much we love our friend and wish them to have the money, we know the money is not theirs. A concept of a higher value comes into play; we know that, at best, it would be unfair to the actual owner of the money if it was not returned to them. Our dilemma is, are we more loyal to our friend or to preserving the notion of justice and fairness? And our own beliefs about the importance of preserving notions of justice and fairness are even more challenged when we are called upon to demonstrate them in front of children, since, as Campbell (2003) states: *students learn lessons about morality through their experiences with teachers* (2003, p.23).

Audi (2007) suggests that when we think of value in this way it is because we are considering something that we feel positive about, and indeed, something that may generally seem to increase wellbeing not only for ourselves but for everyone. That is, just as we may feel we would deliberately act in one way, rather than another, so too we may choose one action above another because we believe it to be for the best. What is challenging in this situation is that we are being required to act in an intrinsically good way not an instrumentally good one. That is, not what is expediently or conveniently good – but what is good because it is the right thing to do.

One of the challenges of living in a diverse society such as the UK is the idea that diversity brings with it multiple understandings of what might be intrinsically good or valuable. However, consider Audi's (2007) suggestion that one of the ways we can begin to know what is intrinsically good and therefore valuable is if it is something that contributes to everyone's wellbeing. In turn, we can know what is promoting wellbeing for everyone because it is based in those things we can agree on as being universally good, things that may be deemed as being essential for everyone – that everyone needs to be able to flourish, thrive or achieve wellbeing. Such things may, for example, be concrete things like food and shelter. They may also be abstract values such as liberty, living in a just society, knowing we will be treated fairly. Most societies also regard education and possibly worthwhile pursuits – work, for example – as being of value. In the same way, we may also agree on things that we do not consider as supporting wellbeing, such as hunger, war and homelessness. As Campbell (2003) states: *the moral domain has at its centre knowledge of right and wrong and involves a transcendent universal set of values around issues of human welfare, compassion, fairness, and justice* (2003, p.15).

Key idea: **Divine commands**

What can we use to help us determine how to behave ethically?

Most cultures and societies have a *divine command* system of ethics – that is, knowing what is right and wrong, or how to behave, rooted in a religious belief and guided by the holy or sacred writings of that religion. Many people look to their religion, and the word of the divine as being central to their religion, for guidance or rules and commands about how to live in an ethically correct way.

Most holy writings are seen as being the word of any given religion's divine being and are that religion's guidance on issues of ethics and values. The word of the divine being may be implicit in the writings, as in *most* of the Jewish Tanakha and Talmud, the Christian Bible and the Hindu Vedas, or the divine being may have been part of the direct writing of the scripture, as with the Islamic Quran. As Audi (2007) states in discussing ethical codes: *among the oldest and most widely accepted is the divine command view. It says, in part, that what we morally ought to do is follow the rules laid down by God* (Audi, 2007, p.8). In terms of religion the UK is historically a Christian country and it is possible to trace many of the ethics, values and laws that form a significant part of UK life and society to their roots in Christianity and the Christian holy book, the Bible. However, for some there are at least two challenges to the divine command theory of knowing what is ethically correct. These are: (1) that while many religions will claim that all, or part, of what their divine being commands may have been directly 'given' by the divine being or god, the interpretation of what those commands mean is often done by human beings; and (2) divine commands, which become rules about behaviour, are often tied to particular religions and not necessarily able to be universally adopted by others, unless they become members of that religion. However, if we have a religious faith we probably have a very clear idea of what our faith expects us to do in the 'found £50' situation.

Key idea: **Reason**

> **What are alternative approaches to the divine command notion of knowing what is ethical?**
>
> A further challenge to the notion of basing ethics and values on divine commands came from a Western European movement known as the Enlightenment. For Europe, the seventeenth and eighteenth centuries were times of considerable industrial, scientific, political and philosophical change. As Beales (2005, p.1) states: *no period can outmatch the catalogue of fundamental changes that came to pass during this time.* One of the fundamental changes that took place was a growing belief in the *power of reason* (Hinman, 2003, p.89), particularly in the power of reason to decide on questions of ethics and values, as opposed to the commands of a divine being, particularly as they were being interpreted in Europe by *Christian Churches and their theology* (Beales, 2005, p.1) at this time.

That reason is such a powerful tool for supporting discussions about what is right and what is wrong stems from the notion that it is only through rational scientific enquiry, through seeking unshakeable, objective proofs of what is fact, that we can come to know what is correct. As Hinman (2003) states: *the Enlightenment captured a rising faith in the power of the human intellect, especially through modern science, to understand the world and to provide a meaning to life* (p.89). One of the most influential philosophers of this time is René Descartes (1596–1650), who explored the notion that the only thing I cannot doubt as a certainty is that I think, and that I can do the business of thinking therefore means that I can know I exist: *Cogito, ergo sum* – I think, therefore I am (p.89).

I cannot necessarily be as certain that anything else is, but I can use my ability to think – or reason – to begin to find proofs that other things may also be so. The influence of such ideas on the European approach to science, politics and religion has been profound. It is now a fundamental part of science and politics in Europe and beyond, that what is so and how things should be is sought through using reason. However, having said reason is fundamental to the notions of science and politics, it is not wholly uncontested as the best or sole way of approaching these areas that have a large impact on general societal welfare.

From the notion of the power of reason we have two issues of particular importance with regard to our wider discussions here. Firstly, up until particularly the eighteenth century in Europe, politics – in terms of those who govern the country and make the laws – and religion were closely allied. From the Enlightenment onwards the two have become increasingly separate. In most European countries religion is now seen as something very separate to government. In Europe generally governments are elected by the populace to run the country and make laws based on the notion that it can be decided through reasoned argument, what is thought to be best for the country. However, this is not a global approach to making law and electing governments. It must also be noted that while in Europe there is the notion of the state being secular – or without religious bias – because most countries have a very strong religious past it is still possible to trace many laws to their roots in divine commands.

Critical Thinking Exercise 3

In 2010 the BBC reported that a Lancashire couple hoping to become foster parents for the local authority: *told Lancashire County Council they would not want gay couples hoping to adopt to come to their home* (BBC, 2010a). The couple say that their stance on homosexuality is in line with the teaching of their Christian faith and, as such they *don't believe gay couples should adopt a young child, and they wouldn't let a same sex couple wanting to adopt a child they were fostering interact with that child in their home* (BBC, 2010a). As a result of these views, Lancashire County Council refused to allow the couple to become foster parents. In a similar case in 2010 Derby City Council denied permission to become foster parents to a local couple after they expressed homophobic views (Sanders, 2011).

1. **Analyse** the two ethical stances here. For example, one approach to doing the correct thing is based on what has been decided is a *reasonable* thing to do and the other based on the interpretation of the Christian God's rules about homosexuality.

2. **Discuss** the tensions here between the competing values in this situation.

3. **Articulate** what, for you, is the view that most closely allies with what you believe should happen.

Comment

As we can see from the critical thinking exercise above, it can often be the case that although some nation-states and countries seek to base their law-making on the notion of electing a government who will *reason* what laws are best for the country, many people wish to follow the ethics given to them by their religion in deciding about what is the correct or incorrect way to behave. For many in society there are strong religious influences that impact on wider notions of ethics and values, be they Christian, Jewish, Muslim, Sikh or Hindu. As Fowler and Hertzke (2009) note: e*verywhere one looks, religion and politics appear to be intertwined* (2009, p.15), and the separation of governance and religion in Europe can still bring ethical and value challenges with it.

Key idea: **duty**

How can we use duty as a notion to guide ethical actions?

For Europe reason has become possibly the most predominant way of discussing what should constitute ethical codes and notions of value, in part because reason is seen as being above bias. The answers reason gives in decisions about right and wrong may not be the ones we like, but they can be shown to be those that can be arrived at objectively. They can seem to be beyond whim or personal inclination. As Benn (1998) states: *the true source of moral obligation is reason, not desire. Reason alone can determine my duty, and it is open to all rational beings to submit to what pure practical reason demands* (1998, p.8).

Benn (1998) reinforces the notion that one of the further uses of basing decisions about ethics and values on reason is that it removes the notion of being governed by personal inclination and, therefore, only doing those things we like, or want to do. Further to this, Benn goes on to state that ethics and values are not necessarily about acting in particular ways only towards those we like; they should also provide us with guidance to enable us to behave well *even if we feel little inner sympathy* for particular people or situations, *lacking such natural warmth is no excuse for not acting with their interests at heart* (Benn, 1998, p.8). Taking this approach to ethics and values also provides us with a consistent rule for what to do, both for us as individuals in a range of situations and as a way of providing for a group a consistent approach to situations. *A reason for me to do something is also a reason for you to do the same thing, in similar circumstances* (Benn, 1998, p.24).

Using this notion of reason, Immanuel Kant (1724–1804) developed an approach to ethics that used the concept of duty as being a way of guiding actions. That is, we know what we should do and what is of value, not through our own inclinations, or the command of a divine being, but because it is the thing that should be done *for the sake of duty* (Hinman, 2003, p.176). Not only this, but that we would agree that whatever the action, we would know it to be correct and dutiful because it would be one that could be *willed as a universal law* (p.176). That is to say, the same rule applies for everyone in every similar situation. This rule approach to ethics is known as the categorical imperative. Not only this, but for Kant what we should also help to guide us in knowing what is our duty, is that we should not see others as a means of getting what we want, but rather that all other human beings are as deserving as us.

Therefore, if we apply Kant's approach to our 'found £50' situation, it is quite clear what we should do. We should, first and foremost, use what is our duty to guide our actions, and our duty is to that which has the higher value – in this instance the values of truth and honesty. We might feel tempted to say our loyalty and care for our friend is of higher value and we can argue we have a duty to those too. But if we follow Kant's next two principles we would also have to say that whatever we decide to do must be what everyone can do in this situation, indeed this is what we are modelling to the children: whatever I do you can do too. The third precept, that we should respect others and not use them for our own ends, also comes into play here. In whose long term benefit would it be if we told our friend to keep the money? Are we really doing it for their own good? Or because we have put our own desire for ensuring their friendship, at any cost, above what might actually be in their own best interest?

One of the criticisms of approaches to ethics and values that use reason and notions of duty as a guide is that they are still notions that sit outside humans as being the arbiter of right and wrong. Some critics will say that using reason in this way simply replaces a divine being – something, that is above and beyond humanity – with the idea of reason. Indeed, despite Descartes' claim, we cannot know, without doubt, that reason is any more or less reliable or actual than a divine being.

Key idea: **Consequences**

What do we mean by consequences?

One of the principles that underpins Kant's approach is the idea that ethics and values are about consequences. That is, when we are thinking about ethics and values we are concerned with actions with regard to certain qualities of behaviour, behaviour that has consequences that may have a good or bad effect on others or ourselves. In our 'found £50' situation, we give our response to our friend some thought as we know there will be consequences attached to our answer. Many of us work to ensure the consequences of our actions are those that have the 'all round' best outcome. That is to say, we wish our friend to have their financial situation eased, but we also know that if they keep the £50 this will only be a short-term resolution of the situation, and there may be other consequences if it is discovered we did not attempt to return the money to its rightful owner. We know there will be consequences for our friendship depending on how we deal with the situation and, as part of our consideration of the situation we also know that we can reinforce or harm the value of fairness and honesty, depending on what our response is. We may also feel we harm our own sense of self if we are not true to our own beliefs about how to behave fairly and honestly. For Kant and for those who are concerned about consequences *when it comes to rightness or wrongness, nothing matters but the results of our actions* (Dreier, 2006, p.5).

We also have to consider the notion that the action we feel it is best to take *might have bad consequences and yet be right* (Dreier, 2006, p.6). For example, you may feel you are prepared to upset your friend in terms of the response you give or that you are prepared to go against your own sense of what is of value, but in this situation you may still feel your chosen action is the best thing to do as *all alternative actions [may] have worse results* (Dreier, 2006, p.6). Again, if we come back to Kant, one thing we could use to help our thinking is what would we want others to do in this case? For our actions to be ethically correct and to be of moral worth, we would say that whatever we do in this situation, we would have others do too.

Key idea: **Absolutism and relativism**

What are absolutism and relativism?

As we have already discussed, there can be a notion that because the UK is a diverse society with *differences in culture, education, ethnicity, religion, and lifestyles* (Audi, 2007, p.vii), these differences can lead to division; that somehow, because there is an idea that *different cultures have different practices and moral priorities* (Benn, 1998, p.1) these apparent differences mean it is not possible to know what is fundamentally, or absolutely, right or of value; that, in fact, ethics and values become *only opinions; that what is right for me may be wrong for you* (Benn, 1998, p.10). Indeed, some will go further and say that *moral judgements are really judgements of personal taste, like one's preferences for certain colours* (Benn, 1998, p.13). Audi (2007) also notes that we cannot necessarily know that what we believe is of value, or that the right thing to do is not simply based on notions of our own preference. The strength of what we might call this relativist position, it is claimed, is that it allows for tolerance of a diverse range of ethics and values. However, as we will see when we explore the notions of absolutism and relativism, this presupposes that everything can or should be tolerated even where tolerance can become abuse.

One of the challenges about our example of the 'found £50' is that some of us may have felt we would behave differently relative to the situation. While we might have given different answers to what should be done relative to the two situations discussed, what we all recognize is that underpinning our response to the dilemma is the notion that we all place a value on fairness and honesty and that we have a set of ethical behaviours surrounding how we deal with situations relating to fairness and honesty. In this way, we agree fairness and honesty as absolutes, in that they are things of value and that our ethical code would try to seek to preserve them. Indeed, as we have already noted, when we take the time to explore what different groups in society believe to be of absolute value, there is more agreement than variation. The values that are seen as being unchanging in terms of their worth, whatever the circumstances, are what ethical philosophers call absolutes. That is, for absolutists, if something has value in one circumstance then, whatever other circumstances it occurs in and whoever is considering the issue, the value it has should always be the same. Where variation occurs between groups is not often in terms of what is of value, but is perhaps in the ethical codes that determine behaviour in response to the values being discussed.

To illustrate this point, let us consider the example of termination of pregnancy, or what is often referred to as abortion. With regard to termination of pregnancy some will hold the ethical view that abortion is never the correct thing to do. This is rooted in the absolute notion of the supreme value of human life, that is, that any one human life is as valuable as another and therefore should be treated as being of worth equal to all others. In such instances abortion is seen as absolutely always wrong. On the other hand, others will come from the ethical standpoint that claims while they agree the supreme value of human life, whether or not a woman should have an abortion is relative to whose life we are considering; life is valued, but there may be situations where lives have relative value when one is compared with another. That is, the value placed on the woman's life, in terms of how her life will be lived or the quality of that life if she has the baby, including the knock-on effect keeping the baby may have on the people and family around her, has to be balanced against the putative life of the unborn child – that is to say, the life the child might go on to experience. In a similar way, while most put a high value on human life, judgements about the worth of some lives against others are made in decisions about whether to engage in war or not. Are the lives lost in the war a price worth paying relative to the overall good outcome, or consequences that will occur if the war is won? Or, again, are the consequences of not going to war to ensure lives are not lost, better than the consequences if the war was fought?

The notion of ethical relativism may seem like a helpful response to the idea that there are a number of ways of approaching a situation; however, it is perhaps necessary to be mindful that the relativist notion of tolerance can slip into moral laziness where the failure to address what may seem ethically challenging situations can lead to abuse. Simply put, doing nothing to be seen to be seemingly tolerant may have worse consequences than doing something.

Critical thinking exercise 4

Consider the following idea. In the UK the age of consent for sexual relations is 16. The aim of this law is to protect physically and emotionally vulnerable young people from being preyed on and sexually exploited. Therefore, if it is believed that children under 16 are too young to be able to give consent to engaging in sexual relationships, particularly in relation to having sex with people over the age of 16, then we believe this to be so for all children, not just for children in the UK. How then might we, in relativist terms, respond to instances where, to satisfy

/continued

Critical thinking exercise 4 – continued

their own desires, some people will travel to countries where the laws about the age of sexual consent may be different to those in the UK and allow sex with someone under 16?

1. This is an instance where we can make **observations** about how others will seek to exploit the notion of tolerance for their own ends. You may be able to think of other examples.

2 **Explore** what your responses to these observations might help you understand about those things you hold to be absolutely always right, or wrong, and those things you are prepared to take a more relativist approach to.

3. Can you draw on the ideas you have read so far in this chapter to help you better **articulate** what ideas form part of your own ethics and values?

Comment

In the critical thinking exercise you have just explored you may agree with Benn (1998) when he claims that a situation such as this is not an example of the tolerance of a relativist position but is about failing to face up to what our own ethics and values mean in difficult situations. That is, if we tolerate others indulging in ethical egoism, that is, exploiting a situation to suit our own wishes, are we being tolerant or simply ignoring a situation we would prefer not to confront or have to think about? In this way, we may need to be wary of using the concept of relativism as a way to ignore dealing with challenging issues which, for Benn (1998, p.18) is actually an act of *moral cowardice*.

Again, while relativism may seem to solve some problems and there may be times when we can each go our own ways with regard to ethics and values, when we come together in a professional setting, like a school, for example, this may not be possible. In a school we need to agree to discuss and work together to build a common set of values and beliefs that we will all adhere to and take forward. In this way, the ethics of the institution may be greater than the sum of individual beliefs, values and attitudes.

Critical thinking exercise 5

Campbell states that: *In the moral domain, however, one opinion is not as good as any other ... Overarching principles have been agreed on in our society and within the teaching profession – principles dealing with honesty, fairness, protection of the weak, and respect for all people* (Campbell, 2003, p.15). She goes on to say: *ethics is not simply a matter of private choice or personal satisfaction* (2003, p.16).

/continued

Critical thinking exercise 5 – continued

1 **Analyse** what Campbell means by these claims.

2 **Consider** how Campbell's ideas connect with your own ideas: do you agree with her, does what she states impact on the way you think about your role in school?

3 **Synthesise** your thoughts about A and B and come up with some ideas about how you might tackle situations in school where there are disagreements about ethics and values.

Comment

One of the reasons institutions such as schools need to be able to work towards a common set of ethics and values is because they are microcosms of society as a whole. Schools sit within diverse communities and part of their role is to look out to those communities and consider the needs of the children they are teaching, not only in terms of what the staff believe makes for good teaching and learning and moral values, but what society as a whole expects from schools. Schools are accountable to society as a whole and have certain external bodies – the government, OfSTED inspectors etc. – to regulate this accountability. Schools need to consider their place in wider society in part because they are funded by taxpayers' money and, it can be argued, are responsible to the society they are providing an education for. Therefore, whatever the ethics and values of individual members of that school, they may still have to be cognisant of wider societal ethics – and laws (Audi, 2007).

Key idea: **Virtue ethics – working at being morally good**

Why be virtuous?

In the tradition of Western European ethics, virtue ethics is an approach rooted in the work of the Greek philosopher Aristotle (384–322 BCE). For Aristotle, knowing what to do is about being *concerned with the sort of people we must be if we are to live the good life* (Benn, 1998, p.161; Hinman, 2003). The 'good life' in this context is a life that promotes our own flourishing and realisation of our own goals, while also seeking to promote flourishing of others too – very much what many teachers say they want for the children they teach.

The ethical situations discussed in this chapter may have presented no dilemmas for you; you may be very clear about what you value and how you should behave in any given situation in response to those values. For others, you may still be grappling with how to know what is of value and what is the correct thing to do in any given situation, particularly where you have to consider your own beliefs relative to those of others.

The last approach we will explore, which philosophers of ethics often offer in seeking to find a way forward with these challenges, is through moving away from the Kantian or consequentialist approach, where *for the Kantian, the central question of morality is 'what ought I to do'* (Benn, 1998, p.160), to an approach that considers *'what kind of person ought I be?'* (Benn, 1998, p.160). That is: *what is a morally good person?* (p.160), what do those whom we deem to be morally correct do?

Critical thinking exercise 6

Below is a set of dispositions, or characteristics, Aristotle outlined which he felt we should be concerned to think about, in terms of our own behaviours, to guide us in being *of good character*. Aristotle is concerned that for each of the dispositions discussed we find, in ourselves, the mean or balanced way of acting them out.

Characteristics or disposition	Underplaying the disposition	Mean or balanced approach	Excess or overdoing our actions
Attitudes to others if they have behaved badly towards us	Ignoring them letting them walk all over us	Proper anger forgiveness, understanding	Revenge resentment
Attitude to the suffering of others	Having no feelings about it	Being concerned and seeking to help	Pity, interfering, taking control
Attitudes to our own desires	Denying them	Indulging them so as not to cause harm	Overdoing our indulgence: lust, gluttony, etc.
Attitudes to other people	Exploiting them for our own ends	Respect	Doing whatever they want

(Adapted from Hinman, 2003, p.280)

1 **Experiment** with the dispositions explored above. Think about a range of situations you have been involved in recently and how you acted.

2 **Compare** your actions with what Aristotle explores about taking the middle ground between two extremes.

3 **Synthesise** your responses to points A and B: what do you conclude about yourself in relation to the notion of being of good character?

Comment

One reason Aristotle's approach is so interesting is that in a sense nothing is 'bad' for Aristotle; we do not have to think should I do this or not? We should, instead, think what should be the limits on my actions? Aristotle counsels us to find the mean *that is the middle ground between two extremes* (Hinman, 2003, p.279). In this way, we can take the characteristics that human beings seem generally to have, as a species, and say that what we are looking for is that we act on these characteristics in ways that promote flourishing for ourselves and for others. In reflecting on these ideas, reconsider the characteristics – or dispositions (see p.23) – and what might be the mean way in which we exhibit them in our own actions.

Does any of this matter?

Perhaps in our day-to-day life we can get by with giving less thought to these issues than when we are acting in a professional capacity in the classroom. As Campbell (2003) discusses, since we voluntarily take on board the role of teacher, it may therefore follow that we must accept with it certain obligations with regard not only to thinking about our own ethics and values but also to discuss with others how, as a school community, ethics and values should be dealt with generally: *membership in a profession obligates individuals to adhere to the ethical principles and standards inherent in the technicalities of the profession* (Campbell, 2003, p.12). Further to this, there is a societal notion that those who hold certain positions, for example, that of doctor, teacher, police officer, have a *duty to behave in an ethical manner* (p.12), an ethical duty that *not only includes but also extends beyond the regular moral conduct expected of any person to encompass elements of competence and service ideals . . . sometimes dubbed 'professional virtues'* (p.12).

Conclusion

Throughout this chapter and the rest of the book we will keep coming back to the issues of 'how do I know what I should do?' in any given situation. The book will not tell you the answer, but what it will do is help you feel more confident in being able to assert what you believe to be correct. Campbell (2003) states that we may *not always know with certainty how a particular ethic applies to a specific problem or situation* (2003 p.16), since, as she goes on to argue: *uncertainty and complexity are inevitable aspects of adjudicating between right and wrong in one's personal and professional life* (p.16). Although, having acknowledged this, *complexity does not invalidate the concept of ethical right and wrong* (p.16). That is to say, issues that will need to be dealt with in a school and in the classroom may be complex and multi-layered in terms of the aspects of the issues that need to be considered and the varying approaches different people will bring to exploring the issue. While an issue may be complex, however, it is still possible to begin to find a way forward by thinking through the fundamental ethics and values that underpin aspects of the issue and using them to seek to find a way forward.

In particular this chapter has asked you to:

- ☉ **consider** what is of value to you and the ethics you live your life by;
- ☉ **explore** where your ethics and values have come from; and
- ☉ **analyse** the impact of notions such as divine commands and reason on popular notions of values and ethics.

Further Reading

Audi, R (2007) *Moral value and human diversity.* New York: Oxford University Press.
Campbell, E (2003) *The Ethical teacher.* Maidenhead: McGraw–Hill Education.
Dreier, J (ed) (2006) *Contemporary debates in moral theory.* Oxford: Blackwell.

2 Ethics, values and social diversity

Vini Lander

Chapter Focus

The critical thinking exercises in this chapter focus on:

⊙ **observing** the behaviour or traditions of a group and identifying their values and ethics;
⊙ **challenging** the assumptions we make about certain groups or situations that involve different groups; your position with respect to certain forms of social diversity, for example, racial and ethnic diversity;
⊙ **discussing** social situations or education-based scenarios that help you to think or talk about the contributing factors associated with that situation;
⊙ **imagining** yourself in the position of someone else in the given situations and scenarios, thinking about how you may see things differently from their perspective;
⊙ **articulating** examples of values and ethics you hold or have seen others exercising;
⊙ **analysing** the impact of the ideas you have been thinking about.

The key ideas discussed are: **social diversity**, **the law, cultural values**, **tolerance versus acceptance**, **dominant discourse** and **plurality**.

This chapter is particularly relevant to Teachers' Standards: **1**, **2** and **8**.

Introduction

It is often conversations or discussions about the behaviour or appearance of a particular group in society that draw into sharp focus how our own personal values and ethics mediate our thinking and responses to such debates. These values are formed within the family and the wider institutions that we as individuals engage in. Our values are informed and shaped by our experiences through childhood and throughout our life. The context of our family structure, our age, ethnicity, gender, class and sexuality as well as other factors such as the geographical location of our home and the local social environment we engage in, influence the ethics and values we believe in and uphold.

This chapter will examine how the personal ethics and values we have developed may shape our response to social diversity within education, and the critical thinking exercises are designed to challenge thinking and help identify how ethics and values are used not only to respond to situations but also how they may sometimes be adapted as a result of such a challenge.

Key idea: **social diversity**

What do we mean by social diversity?

Before we launch into the complexity of examining how ethics and values may be similar or dissimilar across a range of groups in society, we need to establish what is meant by the term 'social diversity' and what and who does it include? When people hear the term diversity they can jump to the conclusion that it refers to racial or ethnic diversity; some will assume that it is related to disability and others to gender. The term social diversity is intended and used in this chapter to encompass the following:

- age
- class
- disability
- gender
- language
- race and ethnicity
- sexuality

However, this is by no means an exhaustive list, as we will see later in this chapter, since some of these categories do not directly fall within the remit of equality legislation.

When we think about diversity in terms of these seven dimensions it is not difficult to accept or appreciate the nature and extent of the term diversity and to further acknowledge that the UK is a socially diverse society and always has been. It is how we respond to these different dimensions of diversity that determines how our ethics and values come into play. But also prevalent in the UK's multicultural and multilingual society are stereotypes related to each of these dimensions of diversity, and these may influence our thinking and response. We may have unwittingly incorporated such stereotypes, such as a retired woman is one over the age of 60, sitting at home in her slippers knitting! Whilst this may be an image we have gained from stories and fairy tales, nothing could be further from reality today. Yet such stereotypes may shape our expectations of someone who is in their sixties and challenge our preconceptions and our values. For example, should a woman who is in her sixties have children if science allows it?

Critical thinking exercise 1

Gaye is a teacher and she has just celebrated her sixtieth birthday. The rest of the staff have enjoyed the cakes she brought into the staff room for break time. After Gaye has left the staff room some members of staff start to talk and say things such as, 'Well she should retire now'; 'She may be looking good for her age and doing well for her age but it will all catch up with her'; 'She should retire before it all goes pear-shaped' (this is not a reference to her figure or physical shape!).

1   **Analyse** the assumptions being made in this example.

2   **Challenge** yourself: do you think you make any of these assumptions?

3   **Consider** how we might have come to have such assumptions and do we make the same assumptions about both older men and women?

Comment

In some societies, particularly in Western European countries, there is an assumption that there is some 'golden age' of competence, that somehow our competence and mental wellbeing are determined by age, and that being older is synonymous with slowly becoming incompetent. Yet in other countries and communities older people are respected and their views sought because their age and experience is valued as an asset, for therein lies wisdom that can be sought to guide others. Why can it be assumed that in the process of aging our competence is diminished and of less value? Is UK society overly obsessed with age, particularly in looking young? Do the images of beautiful, young models whose looks are further enhanced in magazines through air brushing influence our attitudes and the value we place on age? Do we value looks over wisdom and do we apply the same stereotypes to both men and women?

Key idea: **The law**

How do personal ethics and values relate to the law?

The acceptable and agreed ethics and values associated with social diversity are usually enshrined within our laws. In Britain until April 2010 there were a number of laws to govern fair and equal treatment of certain groups within our society: for example, the Sex Discrimination Act, the Race Relations Amendment Act 2000 and the Disability Discrimination Act. Each dealt with how discrimination against one particular group was unlawful. It could be argued that if the UK is a democratic society that values freedom and equality, particularly the equality of all groups, then we should not need laws that determine the ethics of how we behave towards

/continued

Key idea: **The law** – continued

certain groups. However, evidence would suggest that our overarching democratic ideals are sometimes obscured or overlooked in the actuality of interacting with some groups or individuals, or by the ethics and values underpinning some institutions. The mere fact that such laws exist may lead us to conclude that the application of the democratic values of equality and freedom from oppression are not realised at a structural or individual level. For example, the statistics associated with the educational underachievement of certain groups of children and the lack of Black and Minority Ethnic (BME) headteachers in school may indicate the presence of other influential and perhaps hidden factors that may impede the realisation of our societal democratic values.

The new Equality Act 2010 which came into force from October 2010 brings all the previous equality legislation into one law and, the public sector equality duty, which came into force on 5 April 2011 places an ethical public duty on all public bodies and institutions such as schools and colleges. As described by the Equality and Human Rights Commission (2011), this public duty states:

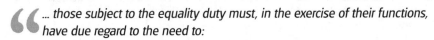 *... those subject to the equality duty must, in the exercise of their functions, have due regard to the need to:*

- *Eliminate unlawful discrimination, harassment and victimisation and other conduct prohibited by the Act.*
- *Advance equality of opportunity between people who share a protected characteristic and those who do not.*
- *Foster good relations between people who share a protected characteristic and those who do not.*

These are sometimes referred to as the three aims or arms of the general equality duty. The Act helpfully explains that having due regard for advancing equality involves:

- *Removing or minimising disadvantages suffered by people due to their protected characteristics.*
- *Taking steps to meet the needs of people from protected groups where these are different from the needs of other people.*
- *Encouraging people from protected groups to participate in public life or in other activities where their participation is disproportionately low.*

(Equality and Human Rights Commission, 2011)

The *protected characteristics* are delineated by the Equality Act 2010 as: *age, disability, gender reassignment, marriage and civil partnership, pregnancy and maternity, race, religion and belief, sex, sexual orientation.* In all, there are nine protected characteristics. Gender reassignment is defined as a specific characteristic to provide protection for transsexual people since it was thought that the phrase *sex and sexual orientation* did not adequately meet the needs of this group.

Critical thinking exercise 2

The Equalities Act 2010 states that persons should not be discriminated against because of age, disability, gender reassignment, marriage and civil partnership, pregnancy and maternity, race, religion and belief, sex and sexual orientation.

1   **Consider** the nine characteristics listed. How many of these characteristics apply to you, your friends or members of your family?

2   **Articulate** any discrimination you or your friends and family may have experienced in relation to these nine characteristics.

3   **Imagine** how people's life experiences and learning and job outcomes might have been different if they had not experienced discrimination.

Comment

The Equality Act 2010 places a general duty on public authorities to ensure there is no unlawful direct or indirect discrimination, harassment or victimisation against those within the protected groups. There is a general duty and specific duties under the Equality Act 2010, which must be met by public sector bodies, which includes state Early Years (EY) settings and primary schools. However, it is worth pausing to consider what is implied about how we value people in that these duties not to discriminate do not extend to the private sector, that is organisations and businesses that do not receive public money.

How do we work with this law in schools?

Below is a table which shows how the Equality Act 2010 applies in EY settings and schools. That is what EY settings and schools must do, or the ethics of how they must behave to ensure the law is being complied with.

General duty	Specific duties
Eliminate discrimination, harassment and victimisation	Publish equality objectives at least every four years
Advance equality of opportunity – for example removing or reducing disadvantage/barriers, equalising outcomes, meeting people's needs; encouraging participation from under-represented groups	Provide information to demonstrate compliance with the general duty through the publication of annual data
Foster good relations between people from different groups who share a protected characteristic and those who do not	Ensure that an equality analysis is undertaken to underscore compliance with the duty

The duty is a proactive duty. In other words, those with responsibility for ensuring statutory requirements in terms of legislation are met within, say, a school would be the governors, the Headeacher and Senior Management. The public sector equality duty comprises the general and specific equality duty and it is the need to advance these duties which leads to the need for equality analysis. This is a means of analysing policies and practices to ascertain whether or not the policies will affect people in different ways and helps the public institution, for example, the school, to ensure they do not build disadvantage into their practices and procedures. The equality analysis is not just a checklist; it involves an in-depth analysis of current practices thinking about equality in the development stages of policies and procedures which could and should involve thinking through the anticipated needs and requirements of all the protected groups and making adjustments proportionately. This is a quite proactive approach to equalities legislation and practice, but it does assume that those who operate the equality analysis have some understanding of the needs and requirements of those in the protected groups.

Critical thinking exercise 3

The local Church of England, predominantly white, village school that you work in has just admitted an Omani girl into Year 5. Anood wears a hijab and covers her arms and legs. Her arrival somewhat 'throws' the headteacher and other members of staff. They seem unprepared for the arrival of a child from a religion with different beliefs to those of Christianity. There are no other children from either a black or minority ethnic background or from a faith other than Christianity in the school. Anood does not want to remove the hijab or uncover her legs, which she would have to, to do PE and to go swimming, since the school has a strict policy on uniform, including its PE kit.

1 **Discuss** whether the school would be acting in a discriminatory manner if they insisted that Anood wore a skirt to school and shorts for PE?

2 **Consider** if the school should have been better prepared for children from another faith group.

3 **Analyse** if the school has been proactive in its general duty under the Equality Act 2010?

Comment

According to the Equality Act 2010 and the associated process of equality analysis, the school should have reviewed its PE, race equality, religion and belief policies against the protected characteristics and anticipated the needs of people from other faiths. Discussing such issues can lead to responses such as: *How many other faiths do we have to consider? We can't make provision for all of them! We don't know what they want or need.* However, such protestations show that some perspectives are being valued over others. What attitudes and values are promoted through these comments? If we leave to one side the fact that the lack of provision for Anood was not compliant with the general duty of the Equality Act 2010, we are then left with comments that encapsulate the values and positions of those who are in the majority within the school and therefore are seen as the most valued. This begs the question, do we only value what the majority in any one situation want and is this an ethically good way to behave? We might consider if we would still feel the majority values and behaviours are the correct ones if the situation was reversed, if a Christian child's needs and wishes were overlooked because the predominant faith in that situation was not Christianity. In the scenario above is embedded the dilemma of how what we want for ourselves must consider the needs of others. In this instance, if Anood's needs are not considered we compromise democratic values of equality and freedom, in order to protect the right of this majority to practise procedures as they always have done, disregarding the needs of another, simply because they are the minority and can therefore be seen as being of less value.

Key Idea: **Cultural Values**

What do we mean by cultural values?

This section explores the notion of culture and what we mean by the term culture. We all belong to a culture, it is not something that is the exclusive possession of those from black or minority ethnic groups, as sometimes is commonly assumed. The notion of culture is inadvertently and unconsciously accompanied by ideas of 'us' and 'them' denoting a better or superior culture and conversely a lesser or inferior culture. This is explored later in one of the exercises you will be asked to complete.

The terms 'ethnicity' and 'culture' often get conflated as if they were one and the same thing. We all have an ethnicity and we all have a culture. Ethnicity is related to people who have similarities in connection to:

> *language, religion, geographical roots (so perhaps physical appearance), and some customs to do with food, dress, family relationships and marriage ... also involves self-consciousness as a group, which may be*

internally generated or at least in part be imposed from outside ... All such boundaries are fluid and cannot be regarded as absolute.

(Gaine, 2005, pp.77–78)

So, we can say that Welsh, or Scottish, or Irish are all ethnicities with a geographical, linguistic but not necessarily a religious connection. For depending on whether I am a Catholic or a Protestant Scottish person the religious affiliation brings with it another dimension of ethnic specificity. For example, we may have people who speak Punjabi, they may originate from the Punjab region of the Indian subcontinent but their ethnicity or ethnic affiliation will depend on whether they are from Pakistani Punjab or Indian Punjab; if from the former they are most likely to be Muslim and if originating from the latter they are likely to be either Sikh or Hindu (although there are Muslims who do live in Indian Punjab). The religious affiliation then confers other dimensions of ethnicity and culture.

The term culture has a broad range of meanings. It can be used to refer to language, customs, traditions and dress, or as the anthropological definition used by Lewis cited in Husbands (1982, p.131) describes it, culture is *a way of life handed down from generation to generation providing human beings with a design for living.* In many ways there is an overlap between ethnicity and culture but the exercise below may illustrate the difference between the two.

Critical thinking exercise 4

Sandeep is a teacher in Hounslow, West London, and she says: *I am a Sikh but I was not born in the Punjab, specifically in Indian Punjab. I was born in Kenya. My parents are Sikhs, they were born in East Africa, Uganda and Tanzania to be precise. We follow our religion and the customs associated with being an Indian Sikh. My father has a turban, my mother has long hair which she arranges in a bun, I cut my hair (which is contrary to Sikh teachings and beliefs), but I still attend family functions such as weddings which are in the Gurdwara [Sikh place of worship] and I enjoy dancing to bhangara music but equally I also like the Beatles, JLS, etc. I have always lived in England since the age of four. I don't remember Kenya. I know my nationality is British because I hold a British passport.*

1　**Consider** how Sandeep might define her ethnicity, is she Kenyan, British, or British-Indian, or British-Sikh, or Indian?

2　**Explore** what Sandeep's cultural background might be.

3　**Articulate** your own ethnicity and culture.

Comment

On the surface this example seems quite straightforward: Sandeep must be British-Indian in terms of her ethnicity, but yet she does not appear to have been to India (and she was born in Kenya) from the information we have above. In terms of music and traditional family events she seems to associate with this ethnicity; as a Sikh she attends the Gurdwara, but she cuts her hair which does not follow Sikh teachings. When I talked to her she readily admits that by nationality she is British, but does not fully associate with all aspects of her hyphenated ethnicity such as British-Asian, or British-Indian. She feels that she is British-Sikh even though she cuts her hair, but her values and code of conduct, or the way in which she conducts herself in the world, are shaped by the beliefs enshrined in her religion because they were so much a part of how she was brought up. But then there are beliefs and customs related to being Indian that she feels are also part of how she behaves in her personal and professional life. Sandeep goes on to explain that the belief that all people, men and women, are equal is a Sikh teaching and yet she notes how this is juxtaposed by the Indian tradition of finding a husband or wife through possibly an arranged (or nowadays an assisted) marriage, who is not from your village or the same caste (even though she says that Sikhs are not supposed to have castes). She describes her culture as British-Indian. Herein lies the overlap between ethnicity, culture and religion. Sandeep uses her religion to ascribe an ethnicity for herself which is based on a religious affiliation but understands that her culture is Indian in terms of customs, traditions and, to some extent, values and ethics.

Sandeep's story illustrates how some aspects of ethnicity and culture seem to overlap in everyday life and influence the ethics and values she holds. It also demonstrates that popular media depictions of Asian or Indian women draw on the notions of 'Asian culture' as homogeneous or Asian women as subjugated beings, yet Sandeep's story illustrates how she is an independent woman who makes decisions about her life, career and way of being based on a set of values that are drawn from her Sikh heritage, the majority white culture and, to some extent, her religious affiliation. Clearly we can see that an individual's personal values may be culturally derived (Gray and Webb, 2010, p.16).

It may be difficult for some readers to identify with such issues or dilemmas concerning cultural, religious and ethnic origins, let alone think about or analyse where and how their own personal values and ethics have originated from or how they have been formed. There is no doubt that our culture, ethnicity and religion (if we have one) are factors that shape the values we hold and may influence our ethics and the actions we take. These values and any subsequent actions based upon them are part of our everyday decision-making, interactions and inactions. Working in EY settings and schools we need to analyse where our values and ethics may have originated from and consider how they may shape our actions and inactions within the professional context.

Key Idea: **Tolerance**

Tolerance or acceptance?

We hear a lot about tolerance in our society. That it is *good* to tolerate racial, ethnic, cultural, sexual, linguistic, ability/disability and gender differences and the notion that there should be equality of different groups. The word tolerance seems to imply a basic level response to such social diversity, a level of having to *put up with*, as opposed to acceptance, which implies an active embracing of such diversity. So we may tolerate the fact that there is an Equality Law which governs the right of different groups for equality. On the other hand, acceptance appears to be a more positive position, maybe further along the spectrum than tolerance. That is to say, the term *accepting* the principles of equality, the right to equal access and opportunity, for example, signals much more than is meant by the term *tolerance*. Tolerance as a position is a precarious one. At which point, or what small changes need to occur, for tolerance to slip into intolerance? Tolerance is a position where people's values and possibly ethics appear not to change but are maintained alongside a level of tolerance. Only when we accept something new do we actually change our values and behaviours and sometimes it is necessary to use the force of the law to make this happen.

Critical thinking exercise 5

In the last part of the nineteenth and the early twentieth century there was an ever-strengthening campaign to allow women in the UK the same rights and privileges enjoyed by men; including the right to vote and to work. Many tolerated the notions of *female emancipation* and equality in the workplace, but until 1918, when legislation was passed to allow women over the age of 30 to vote nothing changed. Subsequently, equality legislation has continued to be passed up until the present day. It could be argued that the fact that it has been necessary to continue to make laws to support equality for women shows that their status and rights alongside men have not been naturally accepted – if they had, further legislation would not be necessary.

1 **Consider** whether it was men or women in control of making laws and the general day-to-day rules of society in the late nineteenth and early twentieth century. What does this say about who was seen as having most value in society?

2 **Analyse** who had the most to lose in terms of power and control by giving rights to women.

3 **Articulate** what you believe about the situation now – is it accepted that women have equal rights to men, or are they still simply tolerated?

Comment

The exercise above explores a further example of how a group in the majority – in this instance, in terms of legal and cultural power and beliefs – arguably began to share their power and consider the needs of others. However, even a little research shows the move to more equality for women in the UK is the story of a battle. It involves death, imprisonment and, some would argue, torture. It is also argued that had it not been for the First World War, when women had to work to keep the country going, that it would have taken even longer for equality for women to have become valued and for the ethics of behaviour towards women to have changed. Interestingly, with regard to discussions about equality between men and women and girls and boys, more recently the focus has shifted from injustices towards women and girls to the notion that boys are now marginalised, particularly through an education system that causes them to underachieve. The discussion about boys' underachievement has dominated educational debate for some years; some would argue there has been a growing sense of *poor boys* (Wearing, 1994), where boys are being left behind by the girls, whether this is in literacy at primary school or in the attainment of GCSEs at secondary level.

In exploring this issue, Martino (2001, p.172) argues, however, that describing boys as underachieving casts boys as victims and fails to see that girls and boys can be *equally disadvantaged*. Such an approach focuses on boys being underachievers simply because they are boys, rather than because of other situational factors, and seems to value a framework that promotes masculinity and femininity as *oppositional categories* (p.173). That is to say, there seem to be dominant models of what it is to be a male or female that prevail in our society. These models may vary across cultures and national boundaries, but embedded within such models are the values we expect these models of masculinity and femininity may hold and promote. The notion of a certain way or dominant way of being male termed 'hegemonic masculinity' (Renold, 2001) promotes the mode of a male who is competitive in all aspects of life, a male who is not academic or *bookish*; he is cool, street-wise, he is dominant and forceful, good looking and, importantly, *hard, macho and laddish* (Mac an Ghaill, 1994). In the debates about boys' underachievement the notion of boys being left behind may well reflect our values about equality. On the other hand, it may reflect the attitude of some based on the intrinsic value of males as dominant, that a dominant group should not lose their place within the achievement and attainment hierarchy. Yet in the debate about boys' underachievement there is a simultaneous tolerance of hegemonic masculinity, a belief in the need for more male or 'boy-friendly' activities and an unquestioning tolerance of the argument about the feminisation of the primary classroom, all centred on the value that males and females are equal.

We appear to be able to accept the dominant models of masculinity within our society that serve to polarise notions of what it is to be male or female, yet we are less tolerant and possibly some of us do not accept different forms of sexuality because they may conflict with our religious beliefs or the norms that govern our cultural values. On the one hand we can declare that the UK is a multicultural, multiracial, multilingual country, but whether we tolerate or accept this situation is dependent on our personal and cultural values. The debates within the media about immigration, sexuality, travellers, asylum seekers and refugees appear to reveal a reality that is discordant and at times vehemently and diametrically opposed to the values we seem idealistically to articulate as a society.

Key Idea: **Dominant discourse**

What does the term dominant discourse mean?

The term *discourse* is used here in a Foucauldian way. Michel Foucault was a French philosopher who used the term to encapsulate the way in which power played a part in the forms of knowledge produced and how it controls the production of that knowledge (Crotty, 2003). As we have seen above, power can be seen to be the domain of certain groups such as men, such as white men, such as white middle-class men, and in society power resides with the ruling elite, those that make laws and assist in this process.

It is these groups in society overall that shape the discourses in such a way as they dominate through their inclusion in, and underpinning of, the practices of an institution. So teachers engage in a professional discourse that other teachers understand because they know the abbreviations and acronyms, they understand the difference between National Curriculum Level 2a and 2b for English, but a parent from a socially and economically different area is not going to be able to engage in such a discourse. Dominant discourses can shape the curriculum, the structure of assessment and determine who counts and who does not. Dominant discourses can influence beliefs about value and how to behave in ethically good or bad ways. In this way they can have an impact on the values and ethics that apply to education.

Curtis and Pettigrew (2009) explain how successful learning and teaching in a multicultural and socially diverse society is dependent on understanding how we understand difference, diversity and celebrate it with understanding. Some teachers may incorrectly assume that celebration of cultural diversity is about highlighting the exotic aspects of some cultures but this is rather tokenistic, based as it is on the assumption that cultures are homogeneous, for example, that everyone celebrates Eid in the same way across the Muslim world. What if such an assumption was made about Christians celebrating Christmas? Do Anglican Christians celebrate Christmas at the same time and the same way as say the Orthodox Christians in Russia, or Coptic Christians in Egypt? To adopt a tokenistic approach to celebrating cultural diversity merely serves to 'tick the box' for some schools where teachers may believe that they have acted in an ethically good way.

Critical thinking exercise 6

You have overheard the following conversation in the staff room. Two teachers are talking about a Year 6 pupil's sister whose name is Zebedah. They talk in low tones about how Zebedah, a former pupil, was taken to Pakistan to be married and that she was only sixteen. She hadn't wanted the marriage but the secondary school did nothing. One teacher says: *Well it's their culture. You can't interfere can you?* The other teacher says: *Well it is wrong isn't it? We should do something, shouldn't we?*

1 **Analyse** the seemingly competing values of the different groups involved in this situation.

2 **Consider** what you believe is the ethically correct thing to do in this situation.

3 **Articulate** which ethical principles support the view you hold.

Comment

This situation illustrates a dilemma that we should be able to negotiate based on fundamental values of right and wrong. It is wrong to force someone to marry, but it is right to show tolerance and respect for other cultures. If we are not careful we could end up falsely showing respect, or perhaps turning a blind-eye, to a practice that is wrong. Mirza (2009) notes that teachers should act ethically by protecting the human rights of girls in the same position as Zebedah, not unethically through their inaction, which can be explained by showing respect for a culture.

The area of racial and cultural diversity, particularly the area of multicultural and anti-racist education, appears to be an area that tests some teachers' ethics and values. While on the one hand teachers may believe in equality and the worth of each human being, on the other hand the same teachers will articulate why they do not need to engage themselves or the children in their class or school in multicultural education because they do not have any of 'those children' in their school or class. It seems that in this instance geographical location serves to negate the need to demonstrate a commitment to extend pupils' understanding of equality in relation to racial diversity. Yet when some teachers try to develop multicultural dimensions to their curriculum in order to extend their children's understanding of, say, how the Second World War involved the world and how soldiers from the Commonwealth, Sikhs, Muslims and Hindus, fought alongside their white British colleagues, the following scenario may unfold.

CASE STUDY

Stephanie (teacher 1): *What are you doing that for? Why are you bothering with including Indian soldiers in your displays? I don't know, all this multicultural education! It's just indoctrination really!*

Sarah (teacher 2): *So I am indoctrinating the children am I? What about all the children who left school thinking that it was only white soldiers who fought in the two World Wars. Is that a true representation of history?*

Toni (Teaching Assistant): *Well you can take all this 'multi-culti' stuff too far really.*

Sarah: *So what you two are saying is that whilst it's alright to say the right thing about we believe in race equality and all that, you don't really believe it? Are you saying that it is only about ensuring, as we do throughout the rest of the curriculum, that history is about what white people did? Is it about whiteness? Aren't you the people who are the indoctrinators then?*

The term *whiteness* has a very specific definition in the conversation above, and Sarah, the teacher in the above scenario, is a citizenship specialist who applies it appropriately here to refer to the dominant discourse of whiteness which pervades the curriculum (Curtis and Pettigrew, 2009) of some schools and is part of the fabric of some teachers' thinking, actions and inactions despite their well-meaning and articulated positions of tolerating and respecting others. Garner (2007) describes *whiteness* as a dominant powerful discourse of the privileged. He cites Hartigan who says:

 Whiteness asserts the obvious and overlooked fact that whites are racially interested and motivated. Whiteness both names and critiques hegemonic beliefs and practices that designate white people as 'normal' and racially 'unmarked'.

(Garner, 2007, p.5)

In following through this quote, the author shows how powerful groups can use their power to value a particular way of being, over others that, while appearing not to be linked to race or a racialised position, do in effect marginalise or racialise other 'ethnic' groups. Garner (2007) argues that in maintaining this position an unequal power relationship is established where some enjoy privilege and advantage and other groups suffer disadvantage. In the scenario above Sarah is trying to move away from a dominant discourse of history that serves to value by celebrating the valour of only one group whilst omitting other groups, but her colleagues appear not to want her to do this. Stephanie accuses Sarah of indoctrination because she is taking a multicultural perspective on one event in history. Can Stephanie be assumed to show respect for other groups and her colleague through such an accusation? Let's see what happens next.

CASE STUDY

Sarah: *I thought you believed in race equality, Stephanie?*

Stephanie: *But I do.*

Sarah: *Then why are you objecting to this display? Why do you say I am indoctrinating the children? Isn't that what you do all the time by just showing them the dominant story?*

Stephanie: *But I am a good ethical teacher. What are you saying? Are you saying I'm racist? How can I be? Teachers are good people. I am a good person!*

Sarah: *I didn't call you a racist. But think about it, Stephanie. How can you stand there and say you are a good teacher who believes in race equality and then ignore the fact that 3 million Black and Asian soldiers came from the Commonwealth? Is it ethical to ignore this in your teaching? Is it within the letter of the law which encourages us to be proactive in developing good relations between different groups? Is it ethical to say I am indoctrinating the children because I choose to represent the situation as it was? Think about your good ethical teacher self. Are we not here to extend rather than limit children's horizons?*

Sarah walks calmly away.

Key Idea: **Plurality**

When we talk of plurality in terms of there being different groups in society does that mean they do not share ethics and values?

The government states that: *teachers uphold public trust in the profession and maintain high standards of ethics and behaviour, within and outside school* (DfE, 2011c, p.8). There is clearly enshrined within this particular statement a sense of duty to society which is illustrated by the term *uphold public trust.* In the same document the government states that teachers have a duty to treat children well and to protect them, and there is also a need to guard children against the personal beliefs of the teacher. The word *tolerance* is used in relation to the rights of others. The phrase that is interesting in the context of this chapter is that the government describes these as being *fundamental British values* (p.8) which are delineated as *democracy, the rule of law, individual liberty and mutual respect and tolerance* (p.8). However, while fundamental to British values, they are not exclusively 'British' or even belonging to one group in UK society. These notions are fundamental to many countries and communities across the world. That is to say, while, in the UK for example there may be peoples from many classes, cultures, religions and ethnicities, this does not mean they do not hold similar values and seek to behave in ethically similar ways.

In the Parekh Report (Parekh, 2000) the issue of values within a multi-ethnic society was debated. The Report acknowledges that in a society such as that in the UK we need a common set of values that bind us and lend a sense of cohesion to our society and communities. But the Report notes that such values are not meant to be those of the 'numerical majority' (Parekh, 2000, p.53); such values have to emerge from discussion and debate. A distinction is drawn between values that support *democratic dialogue*, that enable us to listen to other viewpoints, that uphold tolerance and mutual respect. Another set of values such as individual freedom to make choices, the equal worth of all humans and equal opportunities and the right to a fulfilling life and wellbeing are, as the Report notes, values that are exclusive to one group or society, and under such values *it is legitimate to ban female circumcision, forced marriages, cruel punishment of children ...* (Parekh, 2000, p.54). The Parekh Report extols the merits of different groups living by their values; as long as they do not *offend against the shared basic values, such differences should be respected* (Parekh, 2000, p.54).

The theoretical field of ethics is not that far removed from the everyday professional life of a teacher. As teachers we adhere to a set of professional values and ethics that are encapsulated within a *Code of Conduct and Practice for Registered Teachers* which is currently implemented by the General Teaching Council for England. The Council governs the professional standards of behaviour expected by serving and pre-service teachers and has the power to issue sanctions against teachers who transgress the Code of Conduct. In September 2012, however, the code of conduct for all teachers, trainee teachers and serving teachers alike will be part of the *Teachers' Standards* (DfE, 2011c). The document outlining these standards has already been referred to above, and just as the document discusses the duty on teachers to uphold certain values it also sets out *Personal and professional conduct* in the following way.

A teacher is expected to demonstrate consistently high standards of personal and professional conduct. The following statements define the behaviour and attitudes which set the required standard for conduct throughout a teacher's career.

- *Teachers uphold public trust in the profession and maintain high standards of ethics and behaviour, within and outside school, by:*
  - *treating pupils with dignity, building relationships rooted in mutual respect, and at all times observing proper boundaries appropriate to a teacher's professional position*
  - *having regard for the need to safeguard pupils' well-being, in accordance with statutory provisions*
  - *showing tolerance of and respect for the rights of others*
  - *not undermining fundamental British values, including democracy, the rule of law, individual liberty and mutual respect, and tolerance of those with different faiths and beliefs*

- *ensuring that personal beliefs are not expressed in ways which exploit pupils' vulnerability or might lead them to break the law.*

- *Teachers must have proper and professional regard for the ethos, policies and practices of the school in which they teach, and maintain high standards in their own attendance and punctuality.*

- *Teachers must have an understanding of, and always act within, the statutory frameworks which set out their professional duties and responsibilities.*

(DfE, 2011c, p.8)

Critical thinking exercise 7

In October 2011 Basildon Council moved to forcibly evict 86 Irish traveller families from their site of abode at Dale Farm. Amnesty International (2011) noted:

We are outraged at Basildon Council's decision to ignore the advice of Amnesty, a wide range of UN and Council of Europe bodies and experts, and other UK-based civil society organisations about the human rights impact of these evictions.

The eviction at Dale Farm represents a failure on the Council's part to comply with international human rights standards on housing and evictions.

1 **Consider** what this incident shows is valued in terms of human rights.

2 **Articulate** the tensions between competing democratic values that underpin this action.

3 **Explore** how you would respond as a member of staff if one of these traveller children was a child at your school?

Comment

In this example members of an established community were torn asunder, leaving some with nowhere to live after the eviction. Much of the controversy surrounding this incident is rooted in the tension between the competing values and ethics surrounding the different modes of living held by the travelling community and the settled community, in this instance, the travelling community being a minority community and the settled community being those whom form the majority of society. What is of particular concern here to organisations such as Amnesty International and United Nations human rights groups is that UK law seemed to fail to protect the homes and families of a minority group. In thinking about your response to this situation, as a member of staff in a local school did you avoid making value judgements about your Gypsy traveller children and uphold the Personal and Professional Code of Conduct as outlined in the Teachers' Standards (DfE, 2011c)?

Conclusion

This chapter has explored how ethics and values can be used and understood in a context of social diversity. In particular the chapter has considered how notions of cultural values, tolerance and acceptance and unchallenged dominant discourses can impact on notions of value and ethical ways of behaving. In discussing these ideas the chapter has sought to engage the reader in:

- ⊙ **analysing** how our values and ethics both personal and professional impact on our decisions and inactions within a professional context;
- ⊙ **considering** how as a teacher and a member of a profession teachers are expected to act ethically and appropriately at all times, both inside and outside the classroom;
- ⊙ **exploring** through the critical thinking exercises within the chapter how you might **challenge** and question the taken for granted thinking and 'norms' that sometimes permeate professional practice.

Further Reading

Curtis, W and Pettigrew, A (2009) *Learning in contemporary culture.* Exeter: Learning Matters.

Lipjhart, A (1999) *Patterns of democracy.* New Haven, CT: Yale University Press

Parekh, B (2000) *The future of multi-ethnic Britain.* The Parekh Report London: The Runnymede Trust.

Wooley, R (2010) *Tackling controversial issues in the primary school.* Abingdon: Routledge.

Zephaniah, B (2001) *Refugee boy.* London: Bloomsbury.

3

What does society want from education – what does it value about education?

Gianna Knowles and Vini Lander

Chapter Focus

The critical thinking exercises in this chapter focus on:
- ⊙ **analysing** what form the underlying principles of the issues being discussed;
- ⊙ **articulating** what underpins your own approach to the issues being discussed;
- ⊙ **challenging** assumptions;
- ⊙ **comparing** a range of approaches and outcomes;
- ⊙ **considering** what ideas provide the most helpful way forward to resolving conflicting situations;
- ⊙ **discussing** the tensions between competing ideas;
- ⊙ **experimenting** with a range of solutions and situations;
- ⊙ **exploring** how issues can be approached in different ways;
- ⊙ **imagining** different solutions to the issues explored;
- ⊙ **observing** how different people deal with different issues;
- ⊙ **synthesising** different ideas to try to reach a way forward.

The key ideas discussed are: **the nature of education**, **how we view children and childhood**, **children's voice** and **teaching children to behave**.

This chapter is particularly relevant to Teachers' Standards: **1**, **2**, **5**, **7** and **8**.

Introduction

 Throughout the world policy makers have increasingly acknowledged the importance of education for promoting economic development and the social and personal welfare of individuals. The right to education is recognized by international human rights conventions and primary education is legally guaranteed in most countries.

(Hallam and Rogers, 2008, p.3)

As the opening quote suggests, education is almost universally recognised as being of value, but there is far less agreement on what education might be said to be and how it should be undertaken.

Thinking Through Ethics and Values in Primary Education

Critical thinking exercise 1

Below are three quotes about education. The quotes come from three different groups, all of whom are concerned with education.

The current government's welcome statement on the Department for Education website states: *The Department for Education is responsible for education and children's services . . . [and] the academies programme which provides schools with greater freedoms to innovate and raise standards* (DfE, 2012).

In writing about Ramsden infant school, OfSTED states this is an outstanding school because it is one where: *Pupils achieve extremely well ... because teaching, the curriculum and the care, guidance and support provided are outstanding and are carefully tailored to pupils' learning needs* (Ofsted, 2009b, p.69).

In 2007 the then Children's Rights Director published a report about children's views of education. It states: *Very clearly, the two best things about school, each given by well over half the children and young people, were being with your friends, and learning the subjects you liked . . . Some of the other best things about school were when you do well at something, having play time, and school trips and out of school activities. Only one person in the whole survey said they couldn't think of any best thing about school to write down* (Morgan, 2007a, p.8).

1   **Consider** what these quotes tell us these groups value about education.

2   **Compare** the values that these groups have in common and any that might be different.

3   **Analyse** how this helps you develop your understanding about what for you are the central or peripheral aspects of the concept of education.

Comment

What we can see from the exercise above is that education can mean different things to different societal groups, depending on what they value with regard to education. However, while we can see there is not necessarily a defining notion of what education is, there are some similarities in what is being discussed. For example, all the extracts seem to suggest that education is about *learning*. The DfE (Department for Education) expresses this but it uses the term *raising standards*, while both OfSTED and the children use the term *learning* more explicitly. Therefore, perhaps not surprisingly, we might begin to agree that one of the things we value in education is learning and that learning may be central to what education is, although we have not yet explored what it is that we value in terms of skills, knowledge and understanding that should be learnt. Similarly, we have not agreed any central ideas about the ethics of how we go about ensuring learning is taking place.

Key idea: **Education**

What is education and what does it do?

While we might not be able to agree precisely on what education is, or what is of value in relation to education, we can possibly come to an agreement about the sorts of things, learning for example, that seem to be central to most notions of education and therefore have value with regard to education. One way of deciding what we value with regard to education is to ask what it is that we want education to do, or phrased slightly differently, what is the aim of education? For example, it would seem from the exercise above that central to the concept of education is the notion that education involves learning; what we might learn we will explore later. Or, as Peters (1970) puts it: *something, of course, must be going on if education is taking place* (1970, p.24). So, what might be *going on* and what of *value* might be going on?

Critical thinking exercise 2

It is often claimed that one of the aims of education is to pass on culture, behaviour, skills and knowledge from one generation to the next. This idea is explored in the following three quotes.

> *Education is, according to some definitions, the transmission of knowledge, value and skills of a culture* (Lal, 2006, p.66).

> *Education aims at: (i) preservation and transmission of culture, (ii) development of personality and (iii) self-realisation* (Puri, 2006, p.59).

Pring (2005) describes education as being what teachers do when they are involved in: *the initiation of young people into what they believe to be worthwhile knowledge, understanding and activities – into a way of life, difficult to enter, which enriches them as human beings* (Pring, 2005, p.13).

1 **Compare** the similarities and the differences in these statements. What do the writers all agree is of value as the aim of education – or what education should do?

2 **Analyse** the assumptions underlying these values.

3 **Illustrate** your thinking by reflecting on how different groups in society might, for example, have different values with regard to what is of cultural value and important knowledge to 'pass on'.

Comment

Having suggested that education is usually regarded as being about learning, it is often generally agreed that the process of education is about passing on, or transmitting, skills, knowledge and understanding that is seen as being of value. However, as Peters (1970) states, education is not only about passing on ideas, but it may also be about helping children to realise the potential within them.

We have begun to explore the idea that one of the things that we value about education is that it passes on skills, knowledge and understanding valued by society. However, as we have seen in Chapter 2, although we use the term 'society' as if it meant one thing, something homogeneous and unified, in reality it is made up of many groups, often with competing ideas and demands. This then raises the question of whose definition or understanding of what society is do we educate children to be part of? Which part of society do we choose as those who should have say over the knowledge and culture we see as being of value and should be passed on? These are important questions to consider, since the knowledge and understanding to be passed on through a medium such as the National Curriculum, for example, not only then dominates what children learn but also only rewards those who learn what is in the National Curriculum. Let us explore these ideas further.

Firstly, the National Curriculum (NC) sets out the subjects and the content of those subjects that must, by law, be taught in every state school. Independent and private schools do not have to teach the NC. Therefore, the NC could be said to be an indication of what is valued, in terms of knowledge and understanding in English, mathematics, history etc., and should, therefore be passed on to children. Secondly, generally achieving well in education in the UK is linked to longer-term benefits, such as employment prospects and, from this, wellbeing in later life. To achieve educationally requires learning the content of the NC, since tests and examinations that lead to future employment are based on the content of the NC. However, different groups in society have different views about what should be in the NC, because different groups value different knowledge and understanding.

Critical thinking exercise 3

One contentious area of the National Curriculum is that of human reproduction and sex education, or Sex and Relationship Education (SRE). Teaching children about human reproduction has been part of the science content of the NC, while schools have not had to teach SRE and parents have the right to withdraw their children from such lessons.

Below are the views of different groups in society about how knowledge and understanding about human reproduction and SRE should be part of the UK education system.

/continued

Critical thinking exercise 3 – continued

In an article entitled 'Is this what you want YOUR five-year-old learning about sex?', the *Daily Mail* discusses some recently produced books to help children understand SRE. The article states: *Among the books singled out in the report is How Did I Begin? . . . which has a cartoon image of a couple in bed in an intimate embrace. It is accompanied by an explanation – using frank and adult terminology – of the act of intercourse – Furious family campaigners have described the material as 'too much, too young' and warn it will encourage sexualisation* (Loveys and Roberts, 2011).

It is the view of the Church of England that: *governors of individual schools must decide but all schools must follow the sex education component of the science curriculum.* They go on to state: *We welcomed the decision to make Sex and Relationship Education a statutory part of the wider curriculum,* adding: *church schools will continue to place sex education within the framework of a Christian understanding of sex and human relationships, which stresses the importance of a faithful marriage as the best framework for sex* (Church of England, 2011).

The Muslim Council of Britain states: *SRE should provide factual information objectively and educate young people to look forward to adult life with a sense of responsibility, accountability and happiness and be ready to build a strong, stable family life* (The Muslim Council of Britain, 2007, p.48).

An article in The Guardian *comments: 'This is not about teaching primary school children to have sex. One of the purposes of sex and relationship education is to try to protect children from abuse,' said Lucy Emmerson, principal officer at the Sex Education Forum* (Shepherd, 2011).

An article in the Daily Telegraph *reports: Margaret Morrissey, from the campaign group Parents OutLoud, said: 'We have been overloading children with information on sex for years and it hasn't stopped record numbers of them getting pregnant and catching diseases.'*

'They think, because they've had a few lessons on the subject, they can cope with indulging in sex. The sensible thing to do would be to wait until these children are grown up and allow them to make their own decisions on sex and relationships.' (Paton, 2010).

1   **Analyse** what different groups in society consider to be the value of teaching SRE.

2   **Consider** the variations in ethical approaches these different groups have with regard to SRE.

3   **Imagine** you are asked for your opinion on the subject by your headteacher – what would you say?

Comment

One of the reasons the content of the curriculum is so contentious is that the nature and content of the curriculum and consequently the school become sites of social reproduction. That is to say, whatever becomes the content taught signifies what is of value and what is going to be passed on and be of continuing value. Therefore, if we go back to the discussion above about SRE, whichever of the possibly competing groups above have their values represented in the curriculum will be the group whose values become the 'correct' and dominant values, and the ones passed on to the next generation. While we have explored this issue with regard to SRE, similar tensions surround what should be the content of the English curriculum, or the history curriculum. In studying English, what books should children read, in history whose version of historical *facts* should be taught?

The second point raised above stated that to be successful in education it is necessary to have learnt the knowledge and understanding within the curriculum. In exploring the link between having knowledge and understanding of the dominant values in society with regard to education gives a child what the French sociologist Pierre Bourdieu called *cultural capital*. Cultural capital can be defined as: *a form of value associated with culturally authorised tastes, consumption patterns, attributes, skills and awards* (Webb et al., 2002, p.x). Further to this, children who come from a home background where they have been brought up in a family who value and have already taught their children values, knowledge and understanding that they will also learn at school, have an advantage over children who may come from a background with different values, knowledge and understanding. For example, if the curriculum and school value stories from certain books and teach as if all children know them, the children that do not will be at a disadvantage and may not understand what is being expected of them. Bourdieu and Passeron (1977) argue that there is an unequal distribution of cultural capital across the social classes which in turn leads to unequal access and outcome. They also note that cultural capital is instilled within the family, societal groups, schools, colleges and higher education and is manifest in language, promoted by selection criteria and social codes. In this way, the group in society who can control the curriculum can continue to dominate what is deemed to be of value and their views continue to be reproduced and become regarded as the correct view.

Key idea: **Children**

What does it mean to be a child?

Education is generally something that is most associated with childhood and being a young adult. Most societies focus education on children – reinforcing the notion that the skills, knowledge and understanding to be learnt needs to happen in the formative stages of life. Or, it might be argued that a society needs to bring out the

/continued

Key idea: **Children** – continued

potential in its young people to ensure their innate skills can be harnessed to benefit society as a whole. That is to say, society needs doctors, teachers, financiers, politicians, etc. and therefore it needs an education system that recognises children who have the potential to be of value to society in competently taking up these roles and an education system that can identify them early and encourage them into these roles. However, it can be argued that in the UK there is tension between competing views of what we mean by childhood and what it means to be a child; that is to say, how being a child is different to being an adult and what *attitudes or ethics* society should adopt in the way it behaves towards children. These ideas are explored in more detail in Chapter 7.

In our exploration of what we value about education and the ethics of how we then go about educating children we do, however briefly, need to begin to discuss what we might mean by childhood – or value as being what childhood should be. Only if we have some idea about what we value in childhood, as being special to children, and how education relates to that, can we think about the ethics of how we deliver education. It is also important to consider these ideas since if education is something that as adults we value it is of even greater importance to children. Education is a significant part of what constitutes the experience of childhood in the UK and, therefore, considerably impacts on children's day-to-day experience of life. The values and ethics children learn at school and about education will also form part of who they are as adults; what they continue to value as they grow up and in turn consider what is valuable in education and an ethical way to go about education for the following generation.

Critical thinking exercise 4

Below is a range of comments from a number of different sources that explore what it means to be a child, official reports on aspects of the school and care system, and comments from children about the actual experience of being a child.

Children embody a state of innocence, purity and natural goodness that is only contaminated on contact with the corrupt outside world . . . Children's purity should be respected and protected in order for them to express themselves freely and creatively (Kehily, 2008, p.5).

Children saw the worst thing about being in care as missing their family . . . Disabled children particularly missed being with brothers, sisters and friends . . . Being bullied by other children for being in care was the most usual way of being treated worse (OfSTED, 2009a, p.3).

/continued

Critical thinking exercise 4 – continued

The number of children recorded by the local authorities as being missing from education and those who were 'lost' to an authority in one year varied considerably. One small authority reported that it had six children whose whereabouts were unknown. Another much larger rural authority had received 1,113 'Children Missing Education' forms in the spring term of 2009 (OfSTED, 2010a, p.9).

People in your family might try to keep the domestic violence a secret, and your mum might think that you don't know it is happening. Maybe, like you, your mum is feeling upset and afraid. She is probably worried about lots of things, and she might not be able to spend a lot of time with you or look after you as much as she would like (NSPCC, 2009).

We love children for all the things we are no longer and often wish we were. We delight in the fact that they, at least, are not cynical or repressed ... Small children are still capable of wide-eyed wonder at what we no longer see ... They are neither jaded nor obsessed as we often are about the situations, but especially the goods, around us. We love the way they look and respond, even while we feel superior. They exhibit freshness where we experience boredom or addiction. And we identify with this lost paradise of wonder because we have been long banished from it (Cross, 2004, p.12).

1   **Analyse** the different experiences of childhood presented in these extracts.

2   **Compare** what the extracts tell us about what is valued in childhood.

3   **Identify** what you value as being an important aspect of childhood and how your values impact on the ethics of how you behave towards children.

Comment

The extracts above highlight the tension between the value adults can place on childhood and the actual experience of childhood, for some children. For adults childhood can seem to be a time of innocence and protection from the responsibilities and complexities of the adult world. However, we need to consider carefully if this is us, as adults, romanticising childhood and being nostalgic for our own 'lost' golden age free of our current worries, and ensure we are being realistic about the lives children really lead. We can see from the quotes from OfSTED that while for many children childhood is a carefree happy time, for others it can be a very different experience, depending on the contexts they are living their lives in. Indeed the view that education in childhood is about *supporting individual development as a natural progress towards adulthood* (Waller, 2005, p.56) can marginalise and ignore the experiences of many children.

Key idea: **Children's voice**

Why should we listen to what children say?

There is no doubt that children are vulnerable: they are both physically smaller than adults and dependent on those around them for their basic needs – food, warmth, shelter, etc. Children may also be emotionally less mature than adults and have fewer life experiences – that is, they do not have the experience to put what happens to them in a wider context, they do not know that life can be lived in more than one way, that there are many possibilities in terms of the way we can go about doing things – that there is more than one set of ethics, for example. Children tend to grow up believing, initially at least, that what those around them at home and school do and say is how things are and how they should be. This places on those in school the additional professional and moral responsibility to consider that the way they are going about education is the best way possible, since it is an act of trust on behalf of the children that what is educationally best for children is the school's priority.

Critical thinking exercise 5

In discussing the value placed on children's contribution to decision-making in UK primary schools over the past 40 years, Cox et al. (2010) make the following comment: *Very largely the story is one of adult decision-making, albeit in a changing context, with different sets of adults making different kinds of decisions at different times. It is a story in which children's perspectives are not so much consciously ignored as not really considered — either in policy, research or school decision-making. There are some signs that at long last those perspectives are being seen as important — at least at the level of rhetoric but only very patchily as yet at the level of practice* (Cox et al., 2010, p.20).

1 **Discuss** what this comment tells us about how we value children's input into the decisions we make about education.

2. Have you **observed** any examples of good practice in settings and schools in terms of children's views being valued?

3 **Imagine** the sorts of decisions that are made in settings and schools that children's views could contribute to. How might listening and valuing children's input improve their educational experience?

Comment

Thinking about childhood also raises the issue of how we view children in terms of what sort of *beings* they are. For example, are children people in their own right with ideas and wishes to be respected – or do they belong to their parents, or the adults around them? Do parents *own* their children and therefore have rights over them (Albertson and Worthington, 2009)? So, for example, what the parents say is right for the child, is what is right for the child. The notion of children as belonging to the adults around them becomes problematic when conflicts arise about some of the ways the child may be being parented and the values and attitudes of how wider society believes a child should be being parented. For example, although parents often talk about children being *their child*, UK laws recognise the right of the parent to parent a child as they wish, but the laws *do not entitle a parent . . . to abuse her [sic] child* (Albertson and Worthington, 2009, p.154). Society recognises that some children need protection from those that look after them. Another dominant view of what it means to be a child is the notion that children are born as empty vessels, or, as the idea is often expressed in the notion credited to the seventeenth-century British philosopher John Locke (Adams and Carfagna, 2006, p.154), that children are a *tabula rasa*, Latin for 'blank slate.' *Locke contended that we are each born without predispositions, and that experience determines the essence of the individual. If you change the experiences, you can change the person* (Adams and Carfagna, 2006, p.196). Simply put, we could express this as: children have the capacity to become whatever we teach them to be.

We have been exploring the notion of how we value children. Are they creatures defined by being the child of a particular family or as unmarked blank slates which a life and personality can be written on to? These two notions of what it is to be a child seem to value children for what they mean to others or for what they can become. An alternative view, as suggested by Cox et al. (2010), is to value children for being agents in their own right, which is indeed what the United Nations Convention on Children's Rights requires of us (this is further discussed in Chapter 7). If we believe in the notion of children having agency, that is having the capacity to be able to make decisions and to be part of decision-making processes, this will, in turn, impact on the ethical approach we take to the process or pedagogy of teaching and learning. That is to say, do we value the child as something unformed until educated, a rather passive notion of what it is to be a child, or as someone who has agency, is active in decisions about their own life and is a partner in the educative process?

Critical thinking exercise 6

An example of good practice in terms of valuing children's input can be seen in the recent review of the family justice system. The report of the review falls under the work of the Children's Rights Director for England:

We asked children for their views on these issues to pass on to the government's Family Justice Review Panel, which has been looking at how the family courts should work in the future. Some of the major findings from the children's views were:

/continued

Critical thinking exercise 6 – continued

Half the children considered that courts do not usually or always make the right decisions for children.

- *Children did not tell us that any of the other possible ways of making major decisions about children's lives were in their view likely to be any better than the courts.*

- *The children saw children's services professionals as overall the best people to make most decisions for children.*

- *They wanted improvements to courts to make sure that decisions are never made by just one person.*

- *They wanted children to be better able to have their say in court decision making.*

- *They wanted major court decisions to be followed up after two years to check that they are still right for the child.*

Going to court could make a child 'scared and afraid of not knowing what was going on', and if a court makes the wrong decision, 'a lot of bad things can happen from one decision' (Office of the Children's Rights Director, 2011).

1 **Consider** what we now know about how the family justice system can be improved and what we would not have known if the children's input had not been valued?

2 **Analyse** what the children's responses reported here tell us about the balanced and rational way children can weigh up a range of arguments and make decisions.

3 **Articulate** the value that listening to children in this case will have in improving children's lives in the future.

Comment

One of the significant criticisms of the notion of listening to what children value and treating children as active agents in making decisions about their lives is the idea that children do not have the knowledge, or emotional and possibly moral experience, to make valid judgments. However, as the example above shows, in this instance listening to what children value with regard to the family justice system has improved the processes and long-term outcomes for children, possibly in ways that adults, working without valuing what the children valued, might have overlooked or even have made worse for the children.

The practical skills and factual knowledge and understanding we value and believe should be taught in schools, that is to say, the *what* of what we are going to teach, is discussed in more detail Chapter 4. Here we are concerned with the complex ethical issue of deciding how best to go about teaching. As we have explored, the ethics that underpin how we work with children throughout their education will be guided by the notion of what we believe being a child to be about. If we believe children are passive in decisions about their lives and education then we may tend to see education as the transmission of skills, knowledge and understanding from us as experts, to them as still learning. This approach is described by Sharma (2010) as: *teacher directed learning* (2010, p.162). That is, the teacher – or setting or school – decide what the child needs to learn and how best it should be taught. Often this approach sees learning as happening in a logical or in a linear way (Brooks and Brooks, 1999) from early childhood through to adulthood. However, as we have seen from the different ideas about childhood above, being a child is itself complex. There is no one experience of 'being a child', everyone experiences their childhood differently depending on the contexts they are born into and, therefore, this approach to learning may not be the most helpful for some children.

Critical thinking exercise 7

In 2009 OfSTED published a report entitled 'Supporting young carers: Identifying, assessing and meeting the needs of young carers and their families'. In compiling the report they *met 50 young carers (37 of whom were caring for disabled parents and 13 for siblings)* (OfSTED, 2009c). The children and young people they talked to were between the ages of 7 and 20 years. In reporting the views of the young carers OfSTED states:

The young carers visited were accepting of their caring role. They saw it as part of normal life . . . However, the young carers identified concerns relating to school and college . . . School responses and the level of understanding and support demonstrated to young carers were variable . . . 'Sometimes I am late for school – they don't remember I'm a young carer. Just put up with the detention' (Young carer).

The young carers talked of their lives being 'hard' and 'stressful'. Caring tasks included the collection and administration of medication, first aid and dealing with family finances. They talked of restrictions on their social lives. 'I don't have anyone back and I don't go out – just say I can't be bothered, it's easier than explaining' (OfSTED, 2009c, p.17).

1. How do the skills, knowledge and understanding already learnt by these children and young people **challenge** assumptions about what schools need to be teaching?

2. **Imagine** these children were asked about what would be most relevant for them to be learning at school. What might they say?

3. **Analyse** the key values that might be in tension between schools that see it as their role to decide how to educate, and children who are active agents in managing large aspects of their own lives.

Comment

While most children have fairly straightforward childhoods, all children are growing up in a complex world and learning how to deal with living successfully within it. The experience of the young carers above does, however, serve to remind us that children can take on responsibility, make decisions and often are very curious and proactive in wanting to *know* things and be part of what is going on around them. Schools that recognise and value these characteristics in children often take what is known as a constructivist approach to learning. This is discussed in more detail in Chapter 6.

Key idea: **Children's behaviour**

What should we teach children about values and the ethics of how to behave?

The current UK government has identified the behaviour of children in schools as an aspect of education policy that it feels to be of significant importance. In particular the government is concerned to put in place measures it sees as helping teachers deal with what might be termed *poor behaviour*. In developing education policy in this area the government has stated that: *a minority of pupils can cause serious disruption in the classroom . . . poorly disciplined children cause misery for other pupils by bullying them and disrupting learning* (DfE, 2010, p.9). It has also stated that children's poor behaviour stresses adults working in schools and children who do behave as expected (DfE, 2010). That the government is concerned with behaviour in schools and is giving advice about how to deal with behaviour tells us that teaching children about the ethics and value of behaving in certain ways is something that UK society, through its government, sees as part of what education should be about. This is perhaps not a surprising idea; what is more challenging, however, when dealing with behaviour in schools is deciding on and agreeing on the ethical issues that underpin this value. For example, whose definition of what is good and bad behaviour do we use and what are ethically correct ways of punishing bad behaviour and encouraging good behaviour?

Before we consider the value of certain behaviours and the ethics surrounding how to teach children to behave, let us just further explore the dominant discourse that behaviour in schools is a problem. Hallam and Rogers (2008) state that while: *In recent years, there has been increasing concern in the developed world that pupil behaviour has deteriorated* (Hallam and Rogers, 2008, p.9), there are conflicting reports about what is happening in schools with regard to poor behaviour. For example, they suggest that the evidence for making judgements about poor behaviour in schools is drawn mainly from one source – the number of children or young people who are excluded from school, noting that: *these data are unreliable as schools vary in the extent to which they exclude pupils, even for the same kinds of behaviour* (Hallam and Rogers, 2008, p.9). What they suggest as a more accurate measure of what is happening with regard to behaviour is OfSTED school inspection reports. These give a more helpful measure as OfSTED visits each school and makes its judgements based on the same criteria, or measures, in each of the different schools. *The number of schools failing an Ofsted inspection because of unsatisfactory behaviour has fallen and violent incidents are rare. Behaviour is only a significant problem in about 1 in 10 schools* (Hallam and Rogers, 2008, p.9). What may be a more accurate assessment of the situation is to consider that while *Some teachers remain anxious about behaviour . . . much of this concern is concentrated in a minority of schools with challenging intakes and poor exam results* (p.9.).

Critical thinking exercise 8

For parents and the majority of well-behaved pupils, good behaviour in school is important to their future success. Pupils have the right to come to school and focus on their studies, free from disruption and the fear of bullying (DfE, 2010, p.32).

Staff should be able to punish unacceptably poor behaviour immediately in the way that they think most appropriate, using their professional judgement and understanding of the child concerned ... They should feel able to remove disruptive children from the classroom, or indeed prevent them from leaving a room where that is necessary to maintain order (DfE, 2010, p.33).

These two extracts are further examples of the government's current discussion surrounding behaviour.

1 **Identify** what are being presented as the main benefits of having good behaviour in schools.

2 **Consider** what *well-behaved* and *unacceptably poor behaviour* might actually mean in the classroom.

3 **Articulate** what for you are *appropriate punishments* for poor behaviour.

Comment

Often, while we may as individuals have what we believe to be very clear ideas about what is good and bad behaviour, when we discuss these in a school context we can find that others have very different ideas. This goes back to our very first discussions in Chapter 1 about where we get our ethics from and how we use them to guide our own behaviour and to judge that of others.

CASE STUDY

Being a teacher in a classroom is a highly complex role. Let us consider a literacy lesson in a Year 3 class. There are 29 children in the class, the teacher and two teaching assistants. Some of the children have English as an additional language (EAL) and one of the girls is in a wheelchair. The class are continuing to work on a story they have been writing; in this lesson they are working in groups to give feedback to each other about developing the characters of the people they have in their stories. You have spent some considerable time planning the lesson to ensure everyone can access the task and find it interesting. You expect that because all the children can access the task that there should be no poor behaviour through boredom or because children are frustrated that they cannot complete the task. Some children have the TAs working with them for support and you expect there to be some talking as it is part of the activity.

You have just set the lesson up when the headteacher comes in and wants to talk to you about an issue. You have to abandon the group you are working with and they go off-task and start talking about something on TV last night. You also notice that one of the teaching assistants seems to be using her mobile phone to send text messages. The girl in the wheelchair tells you that one of the other children is calling her names. You know the child who is doing the name-calling is just about to be taken into care. One of the EAL children has written a stunning piece of work and you want to share it with the whole class as it is just what you want them all to do. Also you feel that sharing it with everyone will boost his confidence. You have just got the class's attention (noticing there is some giggling going on at one table which you intend to investigate in a minute) when the deputy headteacher rushes in to the classroom and says, 'Children, we have a very important surprise visitor. Quick, everyone into the assembly hall.' All the children start talking and some start to line up at the door.

A   Given the different things that happen in the lesson, what would you **consider** low-level disruption and what would be poor behaviour you would want to punish?

B   **Experiment** with a range of responses to the different things that happened.

C   **Discuss** how the behaviour of the adults models to children what is appropriate or inappropriate behaviour.

Comment
Luckily few lessons are like the one just described, although many of you will be thinking *I've experienced far worse*. However, it serves to show that managing behaviour is

a combination of many elements. Firstly, good behaviour is encouraged by planning appropriate learning activities and then it is reinforced by how the adults around respond to the minute-by-minute issues that arise in the classroom – not all of which have an immediately clear response. Even the government, which seems to have made quite a strong statement about good behaviour being of value, recognises that the ethical consideration of how to make this happen is far more contentious. For example, on deciding punishments for poor behaviour the government guidance states that only certain adults attached to the school can punish children and this is at the headteacher's discretion. It also states that the *decision to punish the pupil and the punishment itself must be made on the school premises* (DfE, 2011a, p.5). But, perhaps most interestingly – from the point of view of our discussions – the guidance is aware of the range of ethical challenges that punishing children and managing behaviour gives rise to. For example, punishment: *must not breach any other legislation (for example in respect of disability, Special Educational Needs, race and other equalities and human rights) and it must be reasonable in all the circumstances* (DfE, 2011a, p.5). If you remember our discussion about reason in Chapter 1 you will have noted that here is a direct example of how, in Western Europe, reason is seen as being an important concept that underpins what is deemed to be ethically correct.

Just to help us further, the government develops the notion of what might be reasonable by stating:

> *In determining whether a punishment is reasonable . . . the penalty must be proportionate in the circumstances and that account must be taken of the pupil's age, any special educational needs or disability they may have, and any religious requirements affecting them.*

(DfE, 2011a, p.5)

The guidance also notes that children can behave poorly for a number of reasons and not just because they are disobedient or seem to be choosing to be naughty. The guidance recognises that poor behaviour may be a symptom or response to other things happening in a child's life, that is *whether continuing disruptive behaviour might be the result of unmet educational or other needs. At this point, the school should consider whether a multi-agency assessment is necessary* (p.5). And the guidance is quite clear that corporal punishment – that is, hitting or striking a child – is illegal (p.5).

In terms of offering ideas on what is regarded as good or bad behaviour in a classroom and how that behaviour should be managed, our discussion may not have provided us with much practical support. However, what we do know is that, as we have already discussed, rules about behaviour and how to behave are complex and, therefore, need to be discussed in the context of the schools we are working in. This is further explored in Chapter 6.

Conclusion

In this chapter we have explored the idea that the notion of education seems to be a fairly universal concept, but what individuals and different groups in society mean when they seek to put education into practice can vary greatly. Similarly, many seem to feel education is of value, particularly for children, but again, there are many differences in the way children and childhood can be viewed. Following these discussions, we have also explored how teaching children to behave is often viewed as a core function of education, but finding a consensus about what good behaviour might be and how it might be taught is again not straightforward. While this chapter has raised these issues it is the reader who must:

- ⊙ **analyse** what is of personal value in the concepts discussed;
- ⊙ **consider** how to approach these issues in the classroom in a way that can be defended ethically; and
- ⊙ having **explored** a personal approach to these ideas, to articulate how to put them into practice in the classroom.

Further Reading

Cox, S, Schweisfurth, M, Dyer, C, and Robinson-Pant, A (eds) (2010) *Children as decision makers in education: sharing experiences across cultures.* London: Continuum.

Kehily, M (2008) *Introduction to childhood studies.* Maidenhead: Open University Press.

The Muslim Council of Britain (2007) *Towards greater understanding. Meeting the needs of Muslim pupils in state schools. Information and guidance for schools.* London: The Muslim Council of Britain.

4

Ethics, values and the curriculum

Linda Cooper

Chapter Focus

The critical thinking exercises in this chapter focus on:

- ⊙ **analysing** the nature of our curriculum;
- ⊙ **articulating** your own views on a new curriculum;
- ⊙ **discussing** curriculum structure;
- ⊙ **comparing** different educational approaches;
- ⊙ **considering** curriculum content;
- ⊙ **exploring** the different consequences and outcomes of different curriculum formats.

The key ideas discussed are: **curriculum content, who should be in charge of determining curriculum content, breadth and balance in the curriculum and ensuring the curriculum is up-to-date**.

This chapter is particularly relevant to Teachers' Standards: **1**, **2**, **3**, **4** and **5**.

Introduction

This chapter seeks to explore a range of ideas relating to values, ethics and the curriculum. The term 'curriculum' usually refers to the subjects children learn at school and often includes the skills, such as reading and writing, they also learn. Britain has had a National Curriculum since the early 1990s. The aim of having a National Curriculum is to ensure that all children receive an education comprised of the same skills, knowledge and understanding, irrespective of their social status, gender, race or ethnicity, and therefore have the same opportunities to achieve in their learning. However, the challenge of determining what any curriculum, national or local to an individual school, should be comprised of leads to discussions about which subjects and skills are of value and should be included in a curriculum. It also raises issues such as the ethics of including particular subjects, leaving other subjects out or teaching only particular aspects of some subjects. For example, since 1988 subjects such as English and mathematics have, in the English National Curriculum, been seen as having value over and above other subjects and therefore have been given 'core' status, arguably leading to a concentration on the teaching of those subjects to the exclusion of others, such as geography, for example. Interestingly, science has sometimes also been valued as a core subject, but at other times it has had this status withdrawn. Many have criticised this prioritisation of some subjects above others and would argue about the ethics of valuing a subject such as mathematics, for example, more than a subject such as PE, particularly in a society that is experiencing increasing problems with obesity, as evidence shows: *most children do not exercise enough to keep themselves healthy and prevent obesity* (**www.bbc.co.uk**, 2011). Similarly, as we discussed in Chapter 2, in subjects such as history the curriculum content has been focused on a particular cultural view of history, raising ethical concerns about the breadth and balance of its content.

Having already raised some considerations relating to values, ethics and the curriculum, further points this chapter discusses cover:

- What does a curriculum need to cover in terms of skills, knowledge and understanding?
- Whose version of those skills, knowledge and understanding should the curriculum cover?
- What knowledge and understanding in what subjects should a curriculum cover?
- What basic skills should the curriculum teach?
- Who should be in charge of deciding what the curriculum should cover – the government, the school, the local community, the child?
- Is the curriculum always out of date – is it always teaching what the previous generation thinks is important, or does it really educate for the here and now and the future?

All the above issues will be examined in relation to the National Curriculum (DfEE and QCA, 1999), to which state schools currently adhere, and the new forms of the curriculum that have recently been proposed. The chapter will also consider what the government has stated about its ethics and values with regard to the curriculum in the White Paper *The importance of teaching* (DfE, 2010).

Key idea: **The curriculum**

What does a curriculum need to cover? What subjects, what skills?

Alexander (2010) discusses the difficulties of formulating a 'new' curriculum, stating that the task not only proves to be a political and professional minefield, but a conceptual one as well. Our current curriculum consists of ten subjects, three of which are given 'core status' (to be discussed further in the basic skills section) as well as RE (religious education) and the non-statutory subjects of citizenship, MFL (modern foreign language) and PSHE (personal, social and health education). At present the curriculum sets out the detail of what is to be taught in the form of a *programme of study*, while the attainment targets specify what the children should have learned by the end of each key stage (DfEE and QCA, 1999). To the practitioner, teaching ten subjects might be task enough, however, the burden of curriculum

/continued

Key idea: **The curriculum** – continued

specification does not stop there. The emergence of the Literacy and Numeracy Strategies (DfEE, 1998, 1999) and the subsequent Primary Framework for Literacy and Mathematics (DCSF, 2007) added to the load of the practitioner. This was accompanied by the advent of the QCA (1998) *Schemes of Work*, which provided suggestions for what and how to deliver a great deal of content. They were not statutory, but had a great influence on schools and these, combined with other parallel initiatives, have served to push the National Curriculum further into the background. Many practitioners have been left confused at how to deal with this prescribed and overcrowded set of documents.

The conundrum of the overcrowded curriculum was one of the premises for a curriculum review and a general enquiry into the nature of education in the UK. As a result, in the last couple of years there have been new suggested curriculums proposed by Rose (DCSF, 2009) and Alexander (2010). It is interesting to view their proposals and compare these to our current curriculum.

The National Curriculum: primary version (DfEE and QCA, 1999)	Rose (DCSF, 2009) Independent Review of the Primary Curriculum	Alexander (2010) The Cambridge Review
Core Subjects English Mathematics Science **Foundation subjects** Art and Design Design and Technology Geography History ICT Music Physical Education RE **Also required** Sex Education **Non-statutory at KS1 and 2** Citizenship MFL PSHE	**Essentials for learning and life** Literacy Numeracy ICT Personal Development **Areas of learning** Understanding English, Communication and Languages Mathematical Understanding Scientific and Technological Understanding Historical, Geographical and Social Understanding Understanding Physical Development, Health and Wellbeing Understanding the Arts	**Domains of Learning** Arts and Creativity Citizenship and Ethics Faith and Belief Language, Oracy and Literacy Mathematics Physical and Emotional Health Place and Time Science and Technology

Our present curriculum (DfEE and QCA, 1999) prescribes clearly defined subject areas alongside specific essential 'knowledge, skills and understanding' that children should acquire through a Programme of Study. The knowledge to be taught is then further extended through an articulation of the *breadth of study* for each programme area. Although it emphasises the importance of cross-curricular links, the present curriculum is

---

much more subject-orientated than the frameworks suggested by Rose (DCSF, 2009) and, particularly, Alexander (2010), which specify 'areas' or 'domains' of learning.

Critical thinking exercise 1

Review the three curriculums presented in the table above:

1 **Analyse** the breadth and balance of each of the curriculums – is there anything missing or do they remain overcrowded? Are all the subjects presented above necessary for the primary age range?

2 **Discuss** which curriculum format appeals to you the most and which would be most suited to the primary age range.

3 **Consider** how curriculum format and structure might influence practitioner delivery in the classroom.

Comment

This leads us to ask which is the more successful approach, a subject-orientated framework or one that leans towards cross-curricular study? A subject-orientated curriculum can make for a fragmented and compartmentalised learning experience for young children, while the themed approach can enrich the learning in a holistic manner that respects the developmental level of children in the primary age range. Rose (DCSF, 2009), for instance, does not directly argue against discrete subject teaching but he does state that cross-curricular teaching *encourages children and teachers to think creatively 'outside subject boxes'* (DCSF, 2009, p.15). Detractors of a themed approach suggest that 'subject expertise' can get lost through what is traditionally termed as a 'topic approach' and that children often do not know what subject they are learning about. This, it is feared, can lead to poor-quality, generalised learning outcomes.

Key idea: **Whose curriculum?**

What knowledge and understanding in what subjects should a curriculum cover?

The debate over 'subjects' versus 'themes' appears to polarise educationalists and has been a long-lasting discourse. At present, it appears that the DfE (2010) is likely to favour subject teaching over a cross-curricular approach. Whatever happens it should be apparent that prospective teachers must be well prepared to teach from either approach and be well schooled in the arguments and philosophies behind each viewpoint. What should also be important is that their own subject knowledge and understanding of subject pedagogy should be sufficiently embedded to be able to know what makes each subject area 'unique' for the child. Moreover, and fundamental to this argument here, is the principle that teachers should be able to use their own

/continued

Key idea: **Whose curriculum?** – continued

professional discretion to be allowed to teach in the way that most suits their children. Alexander (2010), in his discussion of this theme, effectively sums up this argument when he declares that what truly matters is not how subjects are labelled but *how well* they are taught in terms of knowledge, skills and understanding.

Critical thinking exercise 2

Consider these viewpoints on knowledge acquisition.

Einstein was once asked how many feet are in a mile. Einstein's reply was, 'I don't know, why should I fill my brain with facts I can find in two minutes in any standard reference book?'

1 **Discuss** whether you think knowledge is now so easily come by through the advent of search engines like Google that it has become a cheap commodity and educationalists no longer need to concentrate on the teaching of facts?

2 **Consider** the meaning of the term 'knowledge'. Is 'knowledge' different to knowing about 'facts'?

3 **Articulate** whether you think the curriculum should detail 'knowledge' to be taught for each subject area or instead concentrate on the 'skills' that are identified with the pedagogy of that subject.

Comment

It could be argued that the teaching of factual information is becoming increasingly unnecessary. It is now so much easier to access knowledge due to the advent of technology that one can gain a vast amount of information on a particular subject through a few clicks of a button. Knowledge retrieval requires such minimal effort that one might be justified in asking why practitioners need to spend any time at all delivering it. It could also be argued that trying to remember large tracts of information is a pointless exercise that requires little ingenuity on the part of the learner and will be largely forgotten, over time, in any case. If we look back on our childhood and try to remember much of the content of what was taught we will not be very successful, for if knowledge is not regularly drawn upon it will be lost. Wray (1999) argues that education places an overemphasis on factual knowledge and that an increased awareness of information should not be the only specified aim for a sequence of work. Wray (1999) also makes the additional point that the information explosion mediated by the internet has made it virtually impossible to select the facts that we consider vital for children to learn and that any type of selection will always be contestable.

Key idea: **Knowledge**

What knowledge should a curriculum teach?

These arguments about the 'knowledge-based curriculum' suggest that we need to consider whether any new framework should concentrate on the development of skills and concepts as opposed to knowledge. Here, emphasis is placed on the promotion of 'skills' associated with each subject and on learning how to acquire knowledge rather than the knowledge itself. In the current National Curriculum (DfEE and QCA, 1999) children are required to develop skills and concepts as well as knowledge. So ICT is associated with the skill of 'making things happen' (DfEE and QCA, 1999), which could eventually develop into the adult ability of being able to program a computer.

It is thought that skills combine *contemporary relevance, future flexibility and hands on experience* (Alexander, 2010, p.249). Indeed, Rose (DCSF, 2009) views skills as imperative and his proposed curriculum, which discussed *essential* skills for learning throughout, favoured their development. Rose is not alone in the pursuit of skills. Alternative forms of curriculum that are used throughout the UK also advocate their development. For example, the International Primary Curriculum markets itself as a skills-based initiative, declaring that *the IPC focuses on a skills-based approach, developing adaptable and resilient globally-minded learners* (Fieldwork Education, no date).

Ultimately, both knowledge and skills need to form the backbone of any curriculum; prioritising one over the other makes for a false dichotomy and produces an altogether poorer learning experience. To relegate the importance of knowledge in a curriculum would be somewhat foolhardy. Knowledge is certainly now much more easily acquired via the internet, but there is much more to the acquisition of information than this. Knowledge is there to be questioned, evaluated and synthesised not merely found and accepted. Furthermore, knowledge simply makes learning interesting, it is fun, enriching and fascinating to find out about different subject areas. The CfSA (2011) develops this theme by stating that knowledge has often been misconstrued as the sterile collection of information. Instead it declares that:

 Knowledge should not be presented as 'facts' for children to accumulate, but in a form that enables teachers to construct a coherent knowledge curriculum. The inclusion of the notions of 'understanding' and 'deep learning' are very important.

(CfSA, 2011, p.5)

As well as knowledge, skills and concept development are equally as important. For example, if, in the history curriculum, a teacher merely delivered content, then a good-quality history experience would not be achieved. Just as important here is the development of historical skills and concepts like chronology or cause and effect. Conversely, if these skills were taught without the addition of the fascination of content provided by historical knowledge the learning experience would also be an empty vessel.

Halocha (2002) effectively depicts the co-dependency of knowledge, skills and concepts in his discussion of the promotion of geographical enquiry. Halocha (2002) values the importance of knowledge. He notes that knowledge is not fixed and uses the exemplar of continental drift, the understanding of which was not accepted right up until the 1960s; here new knowledge moved thinking forward, transforming our world-view. The same theory could be applied to the process of global warming today.

Critical thinking exercise 3

The government White Paper *The Importance of Teaching* (DfE, 2010) advocates the importance of knowledge in the forthcoming curriculum. It states: *the National Curriculum should set out only the essential knowledge and understanding that all children should acquire and leave teachers to decide how to teach this most effectively* (DfE, 2010, p.37).

1 **Discuss** who should decide 'what' makes for essential knowledge.

2 **Consider** if there are any possible risks in presenting 'core knowledge'. Are there any occasions in history where curriculum 'knowledge' has been misconstrued or misrepresented?

3 **Explore** the idea of what 'new knowledge' should be included in a curriculum in order to prepare children for the future.

Comment

Halocha (2002) notes that the task of teachers and children is not just to be able to find up-to-date information, but also to spot changes to it and seek explanations for this. In the same text he discusses the fact that while skills are just as important, to teach them in isolation is equally moribund and may mean that the child fails to acquire any context for the learning. For instance, he notes that when teaching the skill of grid referencing children will only see the value of accuracy if they are asked to apply this technique to conduct activities like coding and decoding messages, pictures and routes. Skills and knowledge have to co-exist and are equally important.

Key idea: **Skills**

What basic skills does a curriculum need to teach?

The present curriculum prioritises the core subjects of English, maths and science. However, literacy and numeracy dominate and hold precedence over science owing to the requirement to test in these two subject areas. That primary schools should emphasise basic skills over other areas of learning seems to be an obvious conclusion. Children need to grasp certain essential skills as a foundation for future learning and this has been recognised as one of the main aims for primary educationalists. For instance, the Victorian schooling system almost solely existed to provide children with what is commonly termed the 'basic skills' of the 3 Rs. This theme of 'basic' skills has been a mainstay of education and has been returned to time and again. In the 1970s Prime Minister James Callaghan expressed a well-documented concern that school leavers were not entering the workplace with sufficient basic skills in place to do a 'good job'. The National Curriculum (DfEE and QCA, 1999), as discussed above, retains this basic core. The concern with promoting basic skills to prepare children for the workforce was also a target for the New Labour government. Their National Literacy Strategy (DfEE, 1998) and the National Numeracy Strategy (DfEE, 1999) promoted the same skills that were traditionally associated with the 3 Rs and used similar language in doing so, emphasising the essentially conservative nature of governmental approaches to education.

The White Paper *The Importance of Teaching* (DfE, 2010) continues to fly the flag for the promotion of 'basic skills'. The words *core knowledge, basic skills, basic foundations* and *essentials* can be commonly found in this document. For instance, the White Paper asserts that a new, slimmed down version of the curriculum will allow parents to *hold all schools to account for how effectively their child has grasped the essentials of, for example, English language and literature, core mathematical processes and science* (DfE, 2010, p.38).

It cannot be denied that the acquisition of *fundamental skills* is critical, and without being able to *read competently* a learner cannot adequately experience the joys of learning in a broad range of curriculum areas. It is also simply not good enough that one in five 11-year-olds still leave primary school struggling to read and write at the standard expected of them (DfE, 2010). This figure is actually much higher for so-called 'deprived' pupils – where the incidence of underachievement is as high as one in three (DfE, 2010), despite the avalanche of money poured into the Literacy and Numeracy Strategies to improve standards in these areas.

It could, however, be argued that initiatives like the Strategies have overemphasised the acquisition of basic skills at the expense of a broader enriching curriculum. This has produced a prescriptive and 'strait-jacketed' experience that serves to demotivate children and might, in itself, contribute to underachievement.

It might also be worthwhile pausing at this moment to consider what might be included in the basic skills-set for children of the 21st century. Should the initial skills acquired by children be updated and developed from the traditional 3 Rs? This skills-set, which was common to the Victorian schooling system, was arguably established to provide a basic and essentially non-aspirational education for the masses. Alexander (2009) is in no doubt as to the vital importance played by literacy and numeracy in schools in preparing children for adult life. However, he also calls for educationalists to consider that the scope of these basic skills might be extended beyond reading, writing and arithmetic to *ask what, in the 21st century, is truly 'basic' to young children's education* (Alexander, 2009, p.18).

Morgan (2007b) continues to develop the theme presented by Alexander (2009). He argues that while literacy and numeracy provide an educational bedrock it is no longer enough to focus on just these things as part of the basic curriculum. Morgan (2007b) suggests that the future economy needs young adults who are innovative, flexible, creative and who have high levels of emotional and social intelligence as well as information technology skills. As such, an education system needs to concentrate on producing people who are problem-solvers, who take responsibility, make decisions and who are flexible, adaptable and willing to learn new skills. Morgan (2007b) points to the alternative set of basic skills as advocated by the RSA's curriculum, *Opening minds: Education for the 21st century* (RSA 2008–11), which lists the following themes as their essentials in a curriculum:

- learning;
- citizenship;
- relating to people;
- managing situations;
- managing information.

It is argued that while pupils need to access knowledge they also need to able to be call on a skill set that helps them to operate in the 21st century (Morgan, 2007b). Morgan (2007b) states that educators should enable children to critically manipulate information as a cornerstone of their teaching endeavour. Teaching children to use and manage technology might therefore be considered part of the essential skill set to help them to achieve this aim.

Reviewing the list above, it could be suggested that schools also need to develop socially, emotionally and politically literate young people as a product of a citizenship-focused curriculum. Moreover, should it not be essential that children are educated to be aware of the environmental and cultural issues by which they are surrounded? Should it not be part of the basic skills set that schools generate children who are able to take part in discussion and who can question and contribute to exercises that explore issues affecting their lives. Bailey and Barnes (2008) discuss this theme of educating citizens for the 21st century but look back at the work of Dewey (1916 [1966]) to emphasise their point. Dewey noted that teachers should educate children to be the problem-solvers of tomorrow and explore the range of issues that would be necessary for children to acquire in order to understand the themes that would face them as adults in a modern and changing world. Barnes and Bailey (2008) develop this theme by arguing that the production of children who are environmentally, socially, emotionally and politically aware will have positive benefits on themes such as health, education and crime. They suggest that *learning which has a real bearing on the lives of children is often learning of the highest quality* (Barnes and Bailey, 2008, p.145).

Interestingly, when looking at the recently proposed curriculum that was developed by Rose (DCSF, 2009), the basic skills set that was suggested was very much in tune with the themes addressed above. Though Rose's proposed curriculum has been discounted by the current government, several of the themes suggested in this document still hold resonance and it is worth exploring the absolute essential ingredients for a primary child's schooling, as defined in this document.

Rose (DCSF, 2009) naturally acknowledged the fundamentality of literacy and numeracy, but felt that the role of information technology in the lives of young people should constitute part of what he proposed to be the *core curriculum* or *essentials for life and learning*. Rose acknowledged the increasing *digitalisation* of life and felt that for children eventually to be able to participate fully in leisure, work and citizenship pursuits they need to be fully digitally literate. While children need to learn to write and count, alongside that they also need to be learning to use technology effectively and safely. To ignore the role of technology would be to inadequately prepare children for the adult world. Rose asserts it will become increasingly:

> *important to command ICT skills to prepare for technologies of the future. The foundations for this engagement are best formed in primary schools, where children's enthusiasm for ICT is evident. Moreover, we must avoid raising a population divided between ICT 'haves' and 'have nots', because this would pose a considerable threat to both economic wellbeing and social cohesion.*

(DCSF, 2009, p.69)

Alongside technology, Rose (DCSF, 2009) felt that children needed to have their personal skills sufficiently developed so that they could make the most of the learning opportunities presented to them, and these were also presented as part of the 'essentials for learning'. Teachers spend a great deal of their time developing the personal and emotional skills of children and to ignore this part of their role would be to give a poorer educational experience. For Rose, children needed to be able to identify and manage their own feelings as well as being able to negotiate with others, cooperate, take turns, listen and respond. Rose felt that education provided a *person to person service* (DCSF,

2009, p.73) and that schools should work alongside parents and the community in order to place personal development at the heart of the learning experience.

At this point it is worth evaluating whether a curriculum actually should prioritise a core of essential skills over other subject areas at all. This has been the case for the last decade and it has, it could be argued, resulted in an overall narrowing of the opportunities for learning.

Critical thinking exercise 4

1 **Discuss** what basic skills you think should be included in the curriculum.

2 **Consider** which of the 'basic skill set' should be made indicative of the 21st century.

3 **Explore** the idea that some subjects should be given priority in the curriculum as opposed to giving them all an equal status.

Comment

The curriculum might be viewed as a prescriptive experience rather than a liberating and inspirational framework. It also should be noted that basic skills are not just acquired through the overconsumption of a diet provided by a few subjects. This makes education too polarised and a potentially dull experience. Basic skills alongside a motivation to learn can be developed through a broad and balanced curriculum. Alexander's (2010) new curriculum gives a nod in this direction by not giving dominance to a few subjects but rather presenting eight *domains for learning* in no hierarchical order. OfSTED (2002b) also agrees with this point and, in its analysis of successful primary schools, noted that the highest-achieving schools offered children a broad curriculum. A strong emphasis was placed on humanities, PE and particularly the arts, which served to enrich the learning experience.

Farrell (1999) further develops the theme of breadth when he likens the school curriculum to the conditions of architecture. He refers to the seventeenth-century scholar Sir Henry Wooton who described architecture as *firmness, commodity and delight*. Farrell (1999) contrasts this 'firmness' to the structure of the curriculum, saying 'commodity' refers to appropriateness of the design to the purpose, and 'delight' is the emotional response to the execution of the curriculum. Building on this analogy, he then issues a word of warning against reducing the curriculum to a narrow core of basics when he states that it would be in danger of providing *a one room squat when children should be exploring the Parthenon* (Farrell, 1999, p.48).

Key idea: **Control**

Who should have control over deciding what the curriculum should cover?

Since the imposition of a National Curriculum as a result of the 1988 Education Act, brought in by Margaret Thatcher's government's educational reforms in the late 1980s, schools have become increasingly used to the government and associated governmental bodies, like the recently defunct Qualification and Curriculum Development Agency (QCDA), dictating the look, content and scope of the curriculum. Increasingly, the government's grasp of the curriculum, and through the (albeit short-lived) Literacy and Numeracy Strategies at the end of the 1990s, government guidance on how to teach has tightened by comparison with central control over the curriculum and teaching at the beginning of the twentieth century. Many argue that it is important to have a general, publicly elected body to oversee something as important as what we teach in schools. However, there are just as many who argue that it should be left to teachers as trained professionals who know the communities they are serving to decide what is of value to teach to the children in their school.

Critical thinking exercise 5

While the content of what we teach has become more and more prescribed, the life of the school too has been consumed by central directives. As Alexander (2009) states: *policies are now imposed on teachers at a rate which has made their assimilation and implementation nearly impossible. By one count, between 1996 and 2004 government and national agencies issued 459 documents just on literacy teaching. That's more than one every week for eight years.* (Alexander, 2009, p.11).

1 **Imagine** the impact on planning learning activities if you were having to respond to seemingly constant changes to your teaching.

2 **Consider** how it might affect your confidence about what you believed to be of value in the classroom if you felt you were constantly being asked to change what you were doing.

3 **Analyse** what might be the advantages and disadvantages of having a central agency to make decisions about the curriculum.

Comment

The speed of policy developments can be quite bewildering for the teachers trying to implement them. This delivery of endless policy presents an unwieldy and unmanageable burden on the teacher when trying to keep up to date. Moreover, it can result in a professional confusion when trying to fathom just what might be considered to be best practice. This, in turn, only serves to 'de-professionalise' teachers as they are increasingly instructed in the detail of what to teach and when. This approach seemingly excludes the notion of the presentation of teachers as powerful thinkers who know what is best for their children and who can create a curriculum that meets the unique needs of their class. It could be argued that recent governments have virtually created a manual that tells teachers how to deliver. The CfSA (2011) concurs with this view. This body argues that the top-down design of the curriculum gave little room for interpretation and flexibility and that teachers were not therefore able to apply their own expertise or enthusiasm to their subject specialism. This paper concludes that as a result *teachers lost their capability to construct their own teaching curriculum* (CfSA, 2011, p.6).

Some educational bodies, however, continue to reflect the centralised view of the dictation of the curriculum. For instance, OfSTED (2002b) states:

> *Reducing the curriculum to a statutory minimum, to be adhered to by all schools, and giving scope for a larger part of the curriculum to be determined by individual schools, would on the one hand, intensify the degree of prescription, while on the other, endanger the entitlement of all pupils to a nationally agreed curriculum of similar breadth and balance.*

Alexander (2009) deals with the juxtaposition of state versus a localised determination of the curriculum by proposing an entirely different viewpoint from the one expressed above. While acknowledging that a national entitlement of some kind remains an absolute imperative, Alexander (2009) argues that a 'one size fits all' curriculum does not provide the correct basis to reflect the diversity of British culture today or indeed the different circumstances that are afforded by 17,300 schools that populate this country. Instead, Alexander (2009) suggests that a *national curriculum* should constitute 70% of teaching time while the remaining 30% of time should be dedicated to a *locally* designed curriculum that would allow the schools to tailor their learning to local characteristics and needs.

While Alexander (2009) advocates more curriculum independence for schools, it could also be questioned whether the child should have influence over what is covered in the curriculum. For the UK educational system, which has become so used to having policy centrally prescribed, this concept might present something of a leap of faith in the mind of the teacher. Arguably after years of strategies where the emphasis has been on teaching instead of learning, that the child should have some direction in curriculum coverage might present a conundrum. However, with emphasis on raising the status of the child's voice in school (see Chapter 7), including the child in the arena of curriculum coverage should certainly be a theme worthy of consideration.

Key idea: **Children in control**

Should children be given a role in deciding what the curriculum should cover?

Observing educational systems in Europe can help to give an insight into how the child can be included in this way, and the schooling system in Denmark can be taken as a case in point. While the Danish government dictates a framework for education, as is the case in the UK, responsibility for the detailed content and procedures is devolved. For example, Ashley and Nicholson (2008), during their discussions with Danish educators, asked what a forthcoming programme would look like. In reply, one educator said: *That is not possible. I will meet the students and they will tell me their priorities and my job is to go away and design a programme that meets their needs and the regulations* (Ashley and Nicholson, 2008, p.58).

Another statutory requirement of the Danish National Curriculum is that children should engage in something entitled 'Free Class Discussion' for one lesson per week. In this time both the children and the teacher have to spend time discussing the make-up and approach to be given to forthcoming work (Ashley and Nicholson, 2008). This provides another exemplar of how children can have some sort of influence on the direction of the curriculum.

The approach to the curriculum in Reggio Emilia in Italy is also inspiring in demonstrating how educators there engage very young children in the direction of their learning. Drummond et al. (1997) discuss how teachers there have avoided replicating a teacher-initiated activity-based curriculum based on an exclusive focus on cognition. Instead, the children are given the time and space to develop their own ideas. The curriculum starts from the local interests of the children, which are then developed as integrated projects over a term or a year. This helps to promote an in-depth learning experience where the children are totally engaged in a joint learning experience with both teachers and also parents. Interestingly, the parents are equally valued as part of the learning process and are considered as subject experts who work with the children. The projects inspired by the children provide the very *source* of the curriculum content and produce a powerful common reference point that fosters communication and the development of ideas between adults and children. This serves to promote a *common language* between all parties involved. As a result Drummond et al. (1997) observed an extraordinary level of attainment by the children, which resulted from the freedom to initiate their own individual lines of enquiry and become experts in a field. Drummond et al. (1997) describe the texture and form of clay work of three- to five-year-olds that was equivalent to the attainment levels of many ten-years-olds in England.

Key idea: **A dated curriculum?**

Is the curriculum always teaching what the previous generation thinks is important?

When observing the pace of global change and innovation it feels like a tremendous challenge to produce a curriculum that is durable and will remain current in the ever-evolving cultural and social landscape that children of the 21st century experience. According to Fisch and McLeod (2007), in an informational age the speed of change means that the top ten jobs that were in demand in 2010 did not exist in 2004. Moreover, these authors assert that educationalists are currently preparing students for future jobs that do not yet exist using technologies that have not yet been invented in order to solve problems that we do not even yet realise are problems (Fisch and McLeod, 2007). In the face of these facts, it seems almost an impossible task to produce a curriculum that prepares children for this kind of world.

CASE STUDY

Jason is nine; his mum died when he was five. He lives with his dad, his dad's partner, Jan, his older brother, Daniel, and Jan's daughter, Alisha. On the way home from the after-school club Jason told Jan about the topic on Victorian Britain he was doing at school. He said *we learnt about how Victorian children did the three Rs – that's reading, writing and rithmetic – which is maths really*. He went on to say how Victorian children would also do some geography, history and singing *probably once a week, oh, yeah and girls did sewing!* He laughed. Jason also talked about Victorian children having to do *drill, which is a bit like PE, but you do it in the classroom*.

They sat in the traffic queue and Jason looked at the shops still boarded up after the riots in the summer. Jan said what she had done at school, which seemed to cover about the same sort of things as well, but she said she'd also done cooking while the boys did woodwork – or something; but they did do more PE and went outside to do it. Jason said: *if you think about it, it's about what we do too, we've got computers at school which is different, but we don't use them much*.

Jason had a good sulk when they got in as Jan said she wouldn't buy him the new trainers he wanted, particularly since he'd just had a pair for his birthday last month. Jason talked to his dad on the internet phone; his dad was working away somewhere abroad, Jason couldn't remember the name of where, but he was really interested that for dad it was lunchtime, while Jason was waiting for his tea. Jason told him about the Victorians and some lesson they'd had about knowing who you were talking to on the internet. His dad sighed and told him to be careful and to make sure when they did Florence Nightingale that they did Mary Seacole too.

/continued

CASE STUDY – continued

Jason watched a television programme on the PC that he'd not been able to see the night before; he had a text conversation with his friends to arrange meeting for a hamburger and going to see a movie at the weekend. He had a fight with his brother over using the games console and told Jan that his brother had been swearing at the people he was playing with online. It was always a bit difficult between Daniel and Jan when dad was away; Daniel still hadn't really got used to Jan.

While Jan was taking the stuff out of the dishwasher she was saying how she had just been turned down for new job she had wanted because while she had good GCSEs she did not have them in the subjects they needed. She also said Alisha would be back from uni for the holiday soon, so could Jason move his stuff back to Daniel's room? Jason really liked Alisha; when they'd first moved in she said she'd always wanted a little brother and had really spoiled him. Now she let him have her room when she was away so he didn't have to share with Daniel. Later, eating tea, they all got into a conversation about the bad weather last winter and hoped it didn't happen again so dad could get home OK. They remembered about how they'd had to survive with no electricity for two days and how they couldn't get the car out. Jason went to bed still puzzled about why they had laughed at him when he asked what music Victorians had on their i-pod.

Critical thinking exercise 6

1 **Compare** Jason's experience of school and the life he leads outside school. How does what he does at school link with his experiences outside school?

2 **Consider** in the case study what we learn about aspects of the curriculum that have been seen to be of value for decades and what aspects need to be constantly revised to ensure they enable learners to keep pace with developments in society.

3 **Imagine** you had control over the curriculum. What would you want it to cover and why?

Whatever the revision of the National Curriculum produces in 2012 it is imperative that it is durable and does not simply reflect fads, political agendas or passing educational trends. The CfSA (2011) discusses curriculum content and argues that knowledge that is effective for 21st-century citizens is not the same as for our forefathers. As a result, the content of the curriculum should be considered and expressed thoughtfully so that it is not fixed in a time warp that becomes quickly outdated. It should also be relevant enough to reflect the cultural constructs valid to the children that learn from it; it should not present an obsolete framework that bears little relevance to the lives of our future citizens. A well-constructed curriculum will stand the test of time.

Conclusion

In exploring what a curriculum needs to cover in terms of skills, knowledge and understanding we have explored how discussing these issues raises questions about what is deemed to be of such value that it must be covered in a curriculum. Similarly we have explored the ethics of making decisions about whose version of which skills, knowledge and understanding a curriculum should cover and who should have the final say over a curriculum should it be the government, the school, the local community or the child? Is the curriculum always out of date – is it always teaching what the previous generation thinks is important, or does it really educate for the here and now and the future?

Further Reading

Alexander, R (ed) (2010) *Children, their world, their education*. London: Routledge.
Alexander, R (ed) (2009) *The Cambridge Primary Review research surveys*.
    London: Routledge.
CfSA (Council for Subject Associations) (2011) *Putting subjects at the core of the
    curriculum*.
**Online www.subjectassociation.org.uk/files/webdocs/Cfsa%20subjects%20
    thinkpiece20Mar%202011.pdf**.
RSA (2008–11) *Opening minds*. Online **www.thersa.org/projects/education/
    opening-minds**.

5 # Ethics and values in school organisation – how should schools be led and managed?

Barbara Thompson

Chapter Focus

The critical thinking exercises in this chapter focus on:

- ⊙ **analysing** what form the underlying principles of the issues being discussed take;
- ⊙ **articulating** what underpins your own approach to the issues being discussed;
- ⊙ **challenging** assumptions;
- ⊙ **comparing** a range of approaches and outcomes;
- ⊙ **considering** what ideas provide the most helpful way forward to resolving conflicting situations;
- ⊙ **discussing** the tensions between competing ideas;
- ⊙ **experimenting** with a range of solutions and situations;
- ⊙ **exploring** how issues can be approached in different ways;
- ⊙ **observing** how different people deal with different issues;
- ⊙ **synthesising** different ideas to try to reach a way forward.

The key ideas discussed are: **what we mean by leadership and management, ethics and values in leadership and management, the impact of gender on leadership and management, education and the marketplace, recent value shifts in education, leadership and management and being an effective school**.

This chapter is particularly relevant to Teachers' Standard: **8**.

Introduction

This chapter will ask you to consider how ethics and values relate to management and leadership and to analyse what you understand by all these terms. Specifically, it will explore how ethics and values might be embedded within the management and leadership task and explore whether specific groups of managers and leaders are perceived to manage differently, whether or not this is actually the case. We will explore whether the introduction of the marketplace into the public sector, and specifically into education, has caused a fundamental change in the ways that educational institutions are managed and led. It will be important to consider whether there has been a value shift in the way that leadership and management is performed in the contemporary education marketplace and to explore whether any value shift impacts in the same way upon all those who hold authority positions in educational settings. Before we can consider these issues, however, we need to interrogate what we actually mean by the terms 'manager' and 'leader'.

Key ideas: **Leadership and management**

What do we mean by management and leadership?

In our roles in school we are affected by what leaders and managers do on a daily basis, even though we may not work directly with them all the time. One of the challenges in discussing this topic is to consider whether leaders and managers do the same job or whether their roles are different. Much has been written about this and not everyone agrees. Although sometimes used interchangeably, the terms management and leadership need clarification as, although they have aspects in common, management and leadership are different. The literature related to leadership and management demonstrates the complexity of what is entailed in these two concepts and illustrates a diversity of opinion as to how closely they are interrelated. Often leadership is associated with the interpersonal, or 'people' aspects of the role, while management is more about the organisational and functional dimension of a role.

Dubrin (1995, p.3) argues that in order to understand leadership it is also important to understand how management and leadership differ. He states that:

> *Broadly speaking, leadership deals with the interpersonal aspects of a manager's job whereas planning, organising and controlling deal with the administrative aspects ... leadership deals with change, inspiration, motivation and influence. In contrast, management deals more with maintaining equilibrium and the status quo.*

Covey (1992, p.246), however argues that leadership can be contrasted with management, but is not mutually exclusive. He provides a useful synthesis of what he sees as the similarities and differences between these concepts, noting:

> *Leadership deals with direction – with making sure that the ladder is leaning against the right wall. Management deals with speed ... leadership deals with vision ... with keeping the mission in sight – and with effectiveness and results. Management deals with establishing structure and systems to get those results ... Leadership focuses on the top line. Management focuses on the bottom line ... Management organises resources to serve selected objectives to produce the bottom line ... leadership and management are not mutually exclusive; in fact ... leadership is the highest component of management.*

CASE STUDY

You are in your classroom first thing in the morning getting things ready for the children. The headteacher comes in and gives you back your planning sheets for next week. She expects to see these on a weekly basis, a week in advance. She says the literacy work you are doing looks very stimulating and she is particularly interested in how you are integrating teaching the children for whom English is an additional language (EAL) into the lessons. You have a more general chat about how things are going and two of the children in the class who are of particular concern to you. She says the mother of one of the boys in your class has been to see her to say the father has left the family home; the mother thinks it's just a temporary thing, but the head says to keep an eye on the child. She says how she is looking forward to your input on maths at the staff meeting tonight and asks you how your mum is, as she knows your mum has just come out of hospital. As she leaves to go to the next classroom she says: *Oh, and don't forget reports need to be in by the 25th.*

It's assembly first thing this morning. The headteacher tells the children how proud she is that they have made a huge effort with their recycling scheme and shows them a plaque they have been sent to put up in the school. She makes a big show of handing the plaque over to the premises officer who is standing there with his drill ready. He carries the plaque away and it is indeed up on the wall soon after. She says a bit about what each class did towards winning the award and says she's so pleased the whole school can have extra Golden Time. Later she brings round pencils and key-rings the recycling people have sent and leaves cakes in the staffroom with a thank you note to all the adults who helped make it work.

A **Analyse** the short case study above, thinking about the headteacher. Which of the things she says and does fall into aspects of leadership and which are management tasks?

B **Consider** what the approach of this headteacher might tell us about the values she uses to underpin her leadership and management role.

C **Explore** further what other values you think it is important for a leader and manager to bring to their role.

Comment

Having just reflected on what is entailed in leadership and management roles and how these are carried out, one of the things we can see from this exercise is why it is so difficult to disentangle the notion of leadership from that of management. We can see how this headteacher in terms of management is making sure lessons are planned, individual children's learning is being addressed and the school continues to develop through the staff meeting together to discuss the curriculum. However, almost simultaneously she is demonstrating good leadership qualities by connecting with individual children, parents and teachers as well as leading the whole school and demonstrating what she wants and values for the whole school by successfully involving them in such ventures as the recycling project.

In terms of overlaps, tensions and distinctions that shape the concepts of management and leadership, Kotter (1990) has provided a useful analysis through which these attributes can be discerned (see Table 5.1).

Table 5.1 Attributes of management and leadership

	Management	Leadership
Creating an agenda	**Planning and budgeting:** establishing detailed steps and timetables for achieving needed results, and then allocating the resources necessary for making that happen.	**Establishing direction:** developing a vision of the future, often the distant future, and strategies for producing the changes needed to achieve that vision.
Developing a human network for achieving the agenda	**Organising and staffing:** establishing some structure for accomplishing plan requirements, staffing that structure with individuals, delegating responsibility and authority for carrying out the plan, providing policies and procedures to help to guide people, and creating methods or systems to monitor implementation.	**Aligning people:** communicating the direction by words and deeds to all those whose co-operation may be needed so as to influence the creation of teams and coalitions that understand the vision and strategies, and accept their validity.
Execution	**Controlling and problem solving:** monitoring results versus plan in some detail, identifying deviations, and then planning and organising to solve these problems.	**Motivating and inspiring:** energising people to overcome major political, bureaucratic and resource barriers to change by satisfying very basic, but often unfulfilled, human needs.
Outcomes	Produces a degree of predictability and order, and has the potential of consistently producing key results expected by various stakeholders.	Produces change, often to a dramatic degree, and has the potential of producing extremely useful change …

Source: Kotter (1990, p.6)

However, more recent theories focus less on the difference between management and leadership but concentrate on what are termed *participatory models*, such as distributed and transformational leadership (Harris, 2008). These models, arguably, are collaborative and *open up more spaces for participatory modes of leadership* where leadership roles are held by a number of team members (Blackmore and Sachs, 2007, p.259). Distributed leadership challenges the notion that leadership should be housed in one person, and contemporary studies into school leadership (Fullan, 2001; Harris and Lambert, 2003) argue that leadership roles should be distributed throughout the organisation rather than being invested in an individual. As Fullan (2001, p.1) argues:

It is not about superleaders. Charismatic leaders inadvertently often do more harm than good ... they are role models who can never be emulated by large numbers. Sustained reform depends on many of us, not just on the few who are destined to be extraordinary.

Theories related to distributed leadership argue that it is not enough that those in senior leadership positions merely delegate authority; rather what is needed is the creation of an environment into which people can grow into leadership. Spillane (2001, p.20) provides a vision of organisations where: *Leadership stretches over the work of a number of individuals and tasks are accomplished through the interaction of multiple leaders.* However, the concept of distributed leadership is problematic for a number of reasons and this is linked to what the concept of leadership actually entails. As Cole (2004, p.53) argues, although leaders may empower others and share the *leadership burden*, in the final analysis a leader cannot abdicate responsibility for the group's results. In a situation where multiple leaders are operating simultaneously, the end result may become diffused or lost sight of. A common theme running through theories of leadership is that one of the key tasks of leaders is to produce change (Kotter, 1990), and following on from that, it is important that leaders have the vision to set the direction of that change. In a situation where distributed leadership operates, the question must be asked whether all those in distributed leadership positions would endorse entrepreneurial and visionary discourses. This is a task that *goes beyond planning which is a management process designed to produce orderly results rather than change* (Cole, 2004, p.85). There is a danger that distributed leadership simply becomes delegation of tasks.

Critical thinking exercise 1

Successful leaders and managers need to incorporate the following skills and attributes into their leadership and management style.

Strong goal orientation, or maintaining a focus on what needs to be achieved and arranging resources, including people, in the way that will best meet the targets set (Williams, 2005, pp.2–3).

Transparent integrity, which is about *having clear values and principles about work and people – and sticking to them in day-to-day activity – especially when under pressure* (Williams, 2005, pp.2–3).

Close engagement with others (Williams, pp.2–3) – which includes being able to form relationships with those they are leading and managing in a way that is supportive both personally and professionally, but is not about being a friend. Williams (2005) also comments that *high emotional intelligence* enables successful leaders and managers to communicate with others in ways that make the team feel valued.

/continued

Critical thinking exercise 1 – continued

Contextual perception and resilience, which is the *ability to see higher and wider than the immediate problem or situation and to be able to put issues quickly into perspective and context* and to *find ways around, or through, problems and to come up with new solutions* (Williams, 2005, pp.2–3).

Williams also suggests successful leaders and managers need to have the ability to influence *those above them*, which for classroom teachers is their line manager and for headteachers is the governing body (Williams, 2005, pp.2–3).

1 **Observe** the management and leadership styles of those who lead and manage you.

2 **Analyse** which of the attributes listed above they seem to be using.

3 **Explore** how you respond to being led and managed. What do you value in your leaders and managers?

Comment

You may not be currently working in a school, but the leadership and management attributes listed above apply to all leaders and managers. You may indeed be in a leadership or management position and the exercise will have prompted you to think about the way you go about your role. Throughout this book we have explored in a variety of ways what ethics and values mean in a range of educational contexts and why they are important to consider as part of our personal understanding of what education is about.

Key ideas: **Values and ethics**

What should be the values and ethics of leaders and managers?

From our discussion of values as they relate to leadership and management we can see how some of the concepts that might be said to be of value when it comes to leadership and management are about relationships with others, while also valuing the need to 'get the job done' in terms of ensuring the curriculum is being taught and children are learning, in its widest sense. The ethical side of leadership and management is the actuality of the things that they do and the behaviours they employ in getting the job done. Let us go back to our earlier case study and imagine a headteacher whose leadership and management style runs something like this: the head comes in to your classroom and says: *Here are your plans, I need next week's tomorrow because I am busy at the weekend and won't be able to look at*

/continued

Key ideas: **Values and ethics** – continued

them otherwise. You need to do something about your EAL children, they are not making enough progress. Don't be late for the staff meeting tonight and I hope your mother is OK because I don't want you taking time off to look after her. I can't do assembly today so it's cancelled, but we got that award thing – here, give these pencils to the children. Oh and Jonny's dad has done a runner – if Jonny kicks off send him to me.

It could be argued therefore that in order to carry out the task of management and leadership in an ethical way, underpinning everything should be a consideration of the wellbeing of colleagues and the endorsement of what Thompson (2009) describes as *person centred* management and leadership discourses.

However, leaders and managers have the challenging role of not only looking inwards and working with the diverse community that is their school and ensuring that it is functioning successfully, they must also look outwards and deal with what the government and wider society are telling them they should be doing to ensure their school is functioning well. Therefore, the following sections of this chapter consider some key issues that may impact on the ways that management and leadership is carried out. The first of these is an exploration of whether the ethics and values embedded in management and leadership styles may be gendered.

Key idea: **Gender**

How does gender impact on being a leader and manager?

There is a wealth of literature concerned with debates about whether men and women have different management qualities and styles, and whether they embrace different management values, (Bensimon et al., 1989; Bryman, 1992; Middlehurst, 1997; Collard, 2005; Thompson, 2009). Historically, stereotypical masculine qualities such as rationality and 'toughness' have been seen as being inextricably bound up with notions of what it is to be a manager or leader. Reay and Ball (2000, p.145) argue that although the term 'management' covers a wide spectrum of leadership roles, the very term incorporates notions of hierarchy, power and control; in short, qualities that, they suggest, are commonly seen as 'masculine'. Fundamental to this discussion is the standpoint that, over time, authority has, in the main, been associated with masculinity and *women who manage are insiders with institutional power and authority but who stand outside the male culture [and] are frequently positioned in highly contradictory ways* (Blackmore, 1999 p.107).

/continued

Key idea: **Gender** – continued

In order to succeed in a traditional management culture, Middlehurst (1997) argues that women who become managers develop what are perceived to be masculine ways of managing. Middlehurst says: *As women proceed into management positions, they may undergo a socialisation process whereby they become more like men (i.e. more masculine)* (1997, p.13).

Some time ago, (Ozga, 1993, p.12) argued that 'male' and 'female' management styles differ, and that those styles are predicated on different values. This is because women's role as teachers or managers and leaders in education still tends to be equated with traditional stereotyped views of a domestic role that valorises caring. Acker and Feuerverger (1996, p.401) remind us that:

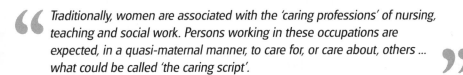

> *Traditionally, women are associated with the 'caring professions' of nursing, teaching and social work. Persons working in these occupations are expected, in a quasi-maternal manner, to care for, or care about, others ... what could be called 'the caring script'.*

There is a danger, however, of identifying all women with uniformly nurturant discourses that seek to care, support and empower. Reay and Ball (2000, p.147) argue that the effects of more 'feminized' management styles may not be particularly far-reaching. They say:

> *Despite the recent trends in management theory which celebrate a 'feminized' management style, the practice of management, especially in educational institutions, remains a paradoxical one for women. While it may be said that these style trends have had some impact on some aspects of management behaviour, it is patently unrealistic to argue that there has been a major transformation in management practices and culture ...*

Blackmore's (1999, p.205) research on leadership also revealed that not all women leaders were necessarily supportive to other women. As she said: *many, but not all, women leaders sought to create safe havens for their colleagues.* The degree to which women managers support their female colleagues, or for that matter each other, is an interesting point.

As we can see, there are lengthy and complex debates related to gender, management and leadership. Some time ago commentators such as Shakeshaft (1989), Noddings (1992), and Ozga (1993) documented differences in men's and women's styles of leadership, positing that a female management style is characterised by ethics of relationships with and care for others. Many early analyses of leadership promote what Court (2005, pp.4–5) refers to as:

> *an oppositional discourse of masculine versus feminine leadership which presented masculine leadership as competitive, hierarchical, rational, unemotional, strategic and controlling, and feminine leadership as cooperative, team working, intuitive/rational, focused on high performance, empathetic and collaborative.*

Reay and Ball (2000, p.147) are somewhat critical of this view and argue that there are doubts as to whether a 'feminized' management style, if it ever existed, was very far-reaching. There are also dilemmas involved in positioning women managers into essentialist roles of universal carers and nurturers (Blackmore, 1999). More recently, Shakeshaft (2006, p.508) has argued that:

> *The literature on gender differences in leadership style is mixed, with one set of literature documenting differences and another reporting no differences. Whether they are different from male administrative approaches, women's leadership styles often include a focus on communication, collaboration, teamwork, inclusiveness, and attention to instructional issues.*

Commentators such as Prichard (1996), Reay and Ball (2000) and Priola (2007) point out that there may be as many differences as similarities between and among women managers, as well as similarities between male and female managers and leaders.

Critical thinking exercise 2

1 **Observe** men and women as they carry out their management and leadership roles.

2 **Consider** whether you think that women perform a more collaborative management or leadership style.

3 **Analyse** what evidence you have for the conclusions you have come up with.

Comment

It is likely that as you carefully consider those around you in leadership and management positions, including your own role in leadership and management, you will conclude that how the person actually undertakes the role will come down to them as an individual, rather than whether they are male or female. As we have discussed, a good leader and manager will demonstrate the attributes, ethics and values we have discussed as being of importance, all of which are attributes that can be exercised irrespective of gender. If we go back to our first case study in this chapter we could as easily imagine our successful leader and manager headteacher as being a man, rather than a woman as the case study states.

The first section of this chapter has considered some key debates related to leadership and management with particular reference to ethics, values and gender. These issues will be returned to later when we look at the ways that leaders and managers work in the current educational climate. Importantly, we need to consider whether the context in which those in authority positions carry out their roles alters what they do and how they behave. Before we can do that, however, we need to understand how the role of education has changed over time and this will help to set the scene for future discussion.

Key idea: **Education and the marketplace**

Is education now valued only for how it can prepare children to work and serve the country's economic growth?

In the 1970s concern was raised by some politicians in the UK and the United States that many public sector institutions, including education, were not paying their way, were poor value for money and were not fit for purpose (Davies, 2003 p.91). There was also concern from some quarters that education should be far more closely related to the needs of employers and the world of work rather than for the more intangible benefits it may offer to people. In 1976, Prime Minister James Callaghan gave what is now a well-known speech at Ruskin College, Oxford, where he launched an attack on the education establishment for *not adequately preparing children for the world of work* and demanding that the then Department for Education and Science should *give a firmer lead* in what went on in schools (Tomlinson, 2005, p.25). Whether or not we believe that Callaghan was right, this was the beginning of far greater government involvement in education, from a position where headteachers and teachers were largely in control of the education given to children in their school to the current climate where, it could be argued, all aspects of education are very tightly controlled and regulated.

Critical thinking exercise 3

As part of its desire to link the purposes and values of education to the demands of the workplace, the UK government made the decision to control the content of the curriculum that would be taught to children. In 1988 it passed the Education Reform Act and introduced the National Curriculum. This is important because it marked the beginning of a change in what teachers do, and, some would argue, the beginning of a reduction in the power of educational professionals to make their own decisions. Ball (1994, pp.48–9) argues that *interventions into pedagogical decision-making lead to an increase in the technical elements of teachers'* work *and a reduction in the professional.* What Ball means is

/continued

Critical thinking exercise 3 – continued

that whereas once teachers, as professionals, would have decided upon the curriculum, now it is decided by the government. It is, as Harnett and Naish (1990, p.11), comment: *that the power has flown away from children, professionals, and LEAs to bureaucrats and politicians at the centre.*

1. **Consider** who should decide on what children are taught and why they should be the people making the decisions.

2 **Explore** the issue from the perspectives of the different agencies involved in making such decisions about education: the government, parents, the children, teachers, etc.

3 **Imagine** you are a member of a school's senior management team. How are you going to reconcile the competing demands from all these different quarters?

Comment

We can see how in the 1980s central government gradually took control of educational functions that had once been carried out by local government and teachers, including control of the curriculum, finance, examinations, teachers' practice and training (Tomlinson, 2005 p.40), Lawton (1980, p.6) argues that the planning of what is taught to children in the school curriculum is: *making a selection of the most important aspects of culture for the next generation. The key question is what is regarded as worthwhile and who makes the selection?* At the same time as central government took increasing control of educational institutions, it also introduced the marketplace into education, which caused a radical change in the working practices of all those who work within all sectors of education and initiated a fundamental change in the ways that schools, colleges and universities are organised, managed and controlled.

With marketplace philosophy came the notion of parental choice. In future children would not have to attend their nearest school but, arguably, parents could make choices about their children's education and funding would follow the student. What this meant, however, was that educational institutions found themselves in competition, rather than co-operation, with each other, which meant a shift in teachers' work from an emphasis on learning and teaching to a focus on competition and entrepreneurial initiatives (Ball, 1994). Schools and teachers found that part of their job was now to attract 'clients' and spending time producing marketing materials in order to publicise themselves. This caused a shift in the work that had to be done by many educational professionals.

One of the effects of schools becoming more like businesses and having to handle their own resources in the education marketplace meant that there was a greater need for management, which was now seen as essential for educational institutions to survive and thrive. This meant that there was a great expansion in managerial roles. Clarke and Newman (1997, p.77) point out that: *The most obvious indicator of the impact of managerialism is the rapid growth in the number of people who have the title of managers.* Ball (1994, p.58) notes the possibility of divisions arising between teachers, (still focussed on learning, albeit of the National Curriculum), and managers, (now focussed on budgets, efficiency and entrepreneurial activities). He argues that management could become a mechanism which *drives a wedge between the curriculum and classroom-orientated teacher and the market and budget-orientated manager, thus creating a strong potential for differences in interest, values and purposes between the two groups* Ball (1994, p.71).

Key idea: **Shifting values**

Has the notion of education as a marketplace changed what is valued in education?

There is an argument that the need to succeed in the current education marketplace has changed the prioritisation of values in education. This is shown in Table 5.2, where traditional values are compared against market-led values of education.

Table 5.2 Changing values in education

Comprehensive values	Market values
Student needs	Student performance
Mixed-ability	Setting
Co-operation with other schools	Competition with other schools
Resource emphasis on 'less able' special educational needs (SEN)	Resource emphasis on 'more able'
Caring ethos	Academic ethos
Led by agenda of social/educational concerns	Led by an agenda of image/budgetary concerns
Orientated to serving needs of local community	Orientated to attracting 'motivated' parents
Emphasis on good relationships as basis of good discipline	Emphasis on extrinsic indicators of discipline like uniform

Source: Adapted from Gewirtz (2002, p.54)

Key idea: **Teacher effectiveness**

How has this value shift impacted on what is the role of the teacher?

One result of an educational culture based on market forces, performance and results is an increased emphasis on the auditing of the work of teachers. As Mahony and Hextall, (2000) put it, the work of teachers and managers in all sectors of education is increasingly controlled by continually shifting policy directives, surveyed by external and internal audit and inspection and judged by performance and outcome. The argument here is not that the work of teachers should not be appraised but that there has been what Power (1994) refers to as an audit explosion, in other words, a continuous appraisal of teachers' work.

Teacher 'effectiveness' is now continuously judged by appraisal schemes, which measure performance against agreed targets (Tomlinson, 2005). Gewirtz (1997, p.225) states that: *clear lines of accountability coupled with appraisal systems effectively manage the work of teachers, ensuring that the values of the performance-driven market are institutionalised to the extent that they penetrate classroom practice.*

Forrester (2003) carried out a study that explored primary teachers' perspectives on what it is like to be monitored in school. Forrester (2005) describes how one teacher, Rosalyn, considered monitoring to be *a time bomb* because she was *so shattered* after a monitored lesson that she *couldn't teach for the rest of the day*. Rosalyn questioned the benefits of monitoring, as she regarded the time spent in preparing for one *monitored* lesson in order to *show herself to be competent* was disproportionate and adversely affected the rest of her teaching for that day (Forrester, 2005, p.278).

It can be perceived that OfSTED inspections further contribute to teacher workload. As well as the amount of evidence that teachers are required to keep, Rosalyn referred to the stress that many teachers suffered as the result of OfSTED inspections. Rosalyn explained that she was *recovering from a one day inspection . . .*; staff had *been in school all over the weekend . . .*; it so happened that only one lesson per teacher was observed, and as Rosalyn remarked: *all that effort for one lesson and we were all ill* (Forrester, 2005, p.278). This burden of work may cause exhaustion and eventually lead to burn-out (Acker and Armenti, p.2004). There is considerable evidence that shows that the roles undertaken, and the hours worked, by teachers have multiplied since the increased value given to education as marketplace. However, what is less understood is the value this has added to the educational experience and outcomes for children.

Critical thinking exercise 4

In an article in *The Guardian* newspaper about how teachers feel about their jobs, Berliner (2011) writes that, talking to them

> [t]ime and time again, they began: 'I love teaching but . . .' or 'This is the best job in the world but . . .' And they were big buts – government targets and interference, senior managers who bullied colleagues to achieve those targets, Michael Gove [the Education Secretary] and Conservative party policy, league tables, OfSTED, bureaucracy, unsupportive parents, declining parenting skills, deteriorating student behaviour, disappearing pensions and lack of respect (Berliner, 2011).

In 2010 *The Independent* newspaper (Kershaw, 2010) reported the following:

> The quality of teaching in schools is too 'variable' and not good enough in half of England's secondaries and in more than two-fifths of primaries, OfSTED's annual report found.

> Up to 400 schools could be tagged as 'underperforming' and will face being taken over if they fail to meet tough new achievement targets set out in today's Education White Paper.

> Education Secretary Michael Gove would not be drawn on the precise number of schools likely to be affected by the measure, which would mean many more schools are likely to be identified as failing.

> While there is currently no target for primary schools, these are expected to fall below the bar if fewer than 60% of their pupils reach level 4 in English and maths and fewer youngsters make two levels of progress between ages five and 11 (Key Stages 1 and 2) than the national average.

> School leaders are also likely to be given unlimited time to scrutinise teachers, scrapping a rule that says they can be formally observed for only three hours a year.

1 **Imagine** you are a parent wanting the best education for your child, what would be your response to the comments above?

2 **Explore** how, as a leader or manager, you would seek to ensure you balanced the views of both the teachers and the government as expressed above.

3 **Anaylse** what both comments tell us about what people value about education and the ethics that underpin how we should go about educating children.

Comment

If the marketisation of education has brought with it a different ethical code, it has also brought, for some, although not all, managers and leaders irresolvable tensions between what they believe education to be and the climate in which they are now forced to operate. Gerwirt's (2002) research provides a clear account of the tensions and challenges faced by a headteacher who has to try to come to terms with working within a different value system from her own. Her story provides a very clear account of the ways in which the values that underpin educational leadership have changed. As we have noted, once the prime concern of teachers and headteachers was the design and content of curriculum and pedagogy, which was determined by education professionals. However, as Gewirtz (2002, p.28) points out:

> Since 1988 headteachers have been responsible for their school's budget and for ensuring that it is managed efficiently and cost-effectively. They now have to make decisions about the appointment, utilisation and the dismissal of staff and the purchase and use of physical resources.

Ms English, the headteacher in question, had had to come to terms with different roles and responsibilities which didn't fit with her own values about education. As she said:

> I do know about working in the classroom ... and I know quite a lot about the curriculum. Now all of that ... the curriculum in particular ... has been removed, not how you teach, but what you teach ... And instead I've been handed huge decisions like sorting out roofs ... or hiring and firing staff ... and I still resent it.

(cited in Gewirtz, 2002, p.38)

Eventually Ms English resigned from her post because she was unable to reconcile contemporary educational market-led values with her own beliefs.

Critical thinking exercise 5

In the current climate where the emphasis is upon what can be measured (performance), these activities are given preference and less visible activities, such as caring for children and colleagues, are less valued (Forrester, 2005, p.274). Ball (2003, p.224) endorses this stance and argues that . . . *performance has no room for caring. While we may not be expected to care about each other we are expected to 'care' about performance.* Reay and Ball (2000, p.151) make the point

/continued

Critical thinking exercise 5 – continued

that certain contexts, or certain periods in history, lend themselves more readily to what may loosely be described as collegiate and collaborative ways of working. They suggest that the late twentieth and early twenty-first century is not one of those times, as the introduction of market forces and new managerialism, has led to workplace cultures *characterised by competition, insecurity and rampant individualism [which are not] conducive to 'caring, sharing' ways of managing by either women or men.* Clarke and Newman (1997, p.73) agree with this standpoint and point out that: *the practice of becoming leaner, fitter and faster organisations has a tendency to produce the worst excesses of 'macho' management (whether practised by men or women).*

1 **Analyse** how your leaders and managers encourage you to be effective in whatever it is you are doing at the moment.

2 **Consider** those aspects of their approach that support you in being more effective in what it is you do.

3 **Explore** the approach you would take towards encouraging others to be more effective.

Comment

In this chapter we have explored leadership and management in education and how aspects of the role of leaders and managers may have changed over time. In particular we have explored the notion that, in recent years, education has become more like a business with, it could be argued, business values rather than some of the values we have explored in previous chapters. It could also be argued that the job of teaching, managing and leading has become tougher, with increasing demands to ensure that prescribed targets are met in the pursuit of continual improvement. However, as always, the central questions that we have to ask ourselves are what we want education to be and what are the ways in which we can balance working within a market-led economy with the values of social justice and behaving ethically. As Ball (2007, p.191) puts it:

We need to struggle to think differently about education policy before it is too late... We need to move beyond the tyrannies of improvement, efficiency and standards, to recover a language of and for education articulated in terms of ethics, moral obligations and values.

Conclusion

As classroom teachers being led and managed by more senior colleagues, or as leaders and managers in schools, whatever the prevailing educational policy of any one government, as individuals we can consider or re-consider what education means to us, and decide upon the values and ethics we want to promote as educational professionals, leaders and managers. In this way this chapter has:

⊙ asked you to **consider** what we mean by leadership and management and the ethics and values that should go with these roles;

⊙ the chapter has also **explored** the challenge for leaders and managers in remaining true to the ethics and values they hold while balancing the needs and wants of the school community and those of government.

Further Reading

Cole, G (2004) *Management: Theory and practice.* London: Thomson Learning
Williams, M (2005) *Leadership for leaders.* London: Thorogood Publishing.
Blackmore, J and Sachs, J (2007) *Performing and reforming leaders: Gender, educational restructuring and organizational change.* Albany, NY: State University of New York Press.

6

Ethics and values in the classroom – classroom management and managing behaviour

Sally Hawkins and Carol Hughes

Chapter Focus

The critical thinking exercises in this chapter focus on:

- **analysing** what form the underlying principles of the issues being discussed;
- **articulating** what underpins your own approach to the issues being discussed;
- **challenging** assumptions;
- **comparing** a range of approaches and outcomes;
- **considering** what ideas provide the most helpful way forward to resolving conflicting situations;
- **discussing** the tensions between competing ideas;
- **experimenting** with a range of solutions and situations;
- **exploring** how issues can be approached in different ways;
- **imagining** different solutions to the issues explored;
- **observing** how different people deal with different issues;
- **synthesising** different ideas to try to reach a way forward.

The key ideas discussed are: **teaching and learning, behaviourism, constructivism and the importance of play, assessing learning, teaching through creativity, the classroom environment** and **behaviour management**.

This chapter is particularly relevant to Teachers' Standards: **1, 4, 5, 6, 7** and **8**.

Introduction

Previous chapters have explored issues relating to values and ethics in education in relation to factors outside the classroom that can have an impact on what happens in the classroom, factors such as the diversity of society, what different groups in society believe the curriculum should cover, what we believe childhood is about and how schools should be led and managed. While these issues are external to the classroom and often widely debated in all aspects of government and society, this chapter explores how we consider these external factors in managing what goes on in our classrooms as a classroom practitioner, be that as a teacher or classroom assistant or cover supervisor. In particular, this chapter will explore ethics and values as they relate to how we might approach teaching and learning, organising our classroom's environment, including how we manage behaviour for learning, and how we seek to provide learning activities that are accessible to all children, whatever their learning needs.

In Chapter 3 we explored what education might be said to be for, or put another way, what the purpose of education is. Having given considerable thought to the ethics and values of what education might be about and, in Chapter 4, to the content of education, or the curriculum, here we focus on how we go about the process of education or, put another way, what the ethics and values of teaching and learning might be about.

Key idea: **Teaching and learning**

Thinking through different approaches to teaching and learning

When we discuss teaching and learning we are thinking about the way we present and teach learning activities in the most effective way to ensure learning is happening. What we value in our approaches to teaching will depend on the age of the children we are working with and what we value in terms of our beliefs about the importance of certain curriculum subjects. We will also have personal views about the best strategies we might use in the classroom to promote learning depending on our own experiences and background. The following critical thinking exercise will help illustrate this key idea.

Critical thinking exercise 1

Imagine you are planning to teach an aspect of mathematics to a group of children. If you are an Early Years specialist, imagine your group of children as being aged four; if you work in the primary phase, imagine your children as being aged seven. There are 25 children in the group.

To ensure the teaching for this group is as effective as it can be, **consider** how the following might impact on your approach to the session:

- the time the teaching session lasts;
- the children's previous experience in this aspect of mathematics;
- the ability range of the children;
- particular learning needs some of the children may have, including SEN, disability and gifted and talented children;
- the diversity of the group, including children for whom English is an additional language, and that your teaching style needs to appeal to both boys and girls.

/continued

Critical thinking exercise 1 – continued

Explore the different ways you might structure the lesson to maximise learning. For example, will you:

- Conduct most of the session from the front of the class, telling the children what to do?
- Set up the learning activity, let the children work in groups and spend your time moving from group to group to ensure learning is taking place?
- Let the children talk and discuss the activity or work in silence?
- Have a range of tasks children can complete depending on their experience and level of understanding, or have one task for all children?

Comment

How you construct your lesson will tell you something about what you value in terms of teaching and learning. It will also tell you something about your ethics in relation to teaching and learning. For example, if you have constructed the lesson so that you are passing your knowledge and understanding on to the children in a direct way from the front of the classroom, then you value the teacher as the expert who has particular knowledge and understanding to impart through their teaching. Or, you may have designed the lesson as being enquiry-based, where you value the teacher as the person who knows how to organise a learning activity where the children can find out for themselves what it is you want them to know. How you have constructed your lesson tells you something about the ethics you use to guide you in the classroom, that is the rules by which you teach. For example, your approach to teaching and learning may be one where the adult in the classroom is very much in control of what is happening. This might include having the learning activity carefully defined as a range of different ability worksheets to complete, or a set of mathematical tasks to work through, having the children working in specific groups you have organised. Or you may have presented the class with open-ended tasks that can be completed in a range of ways, letting the children work in friendship groups and then bring together the main learning points in a discussion, or plenary session at the end. In reality, you probably use a range of teaching and learning approaches, depending on what you are aiming to teach in any particular lesson. Nevertheless, it is important to consider how you are constructing your lessons, as the way you approach teaching and learning does have a bearing on what you value in terms of the role of the teacher and how you believe children learn.

Critical thinking exercise 2

Having given some consideration to your initial thoughts about teaching and learning, this exercise asks you to think through some aspects of what school inspectors value in terms of teaching and learning and the ethics of how teaching and learning should be approached.

The list below outlines some of the aspects of teaching and learning OfSTED will look for when deciding if effective teaching and learning is happening. In overall terms, OfSTED states that: *The most important role of teaching is to raise pupils' achievement ... Inspectors also evaluate activities both within and outside the classroom ... and the impact that teaching has in promoting the pupils' spiritual, moral, social and cultural development* (OfSTED, 2012, p.15).

Inspectors will regard teaching as effective if:

- *teachers' expectations, reflected in their teaching and planning, including curriculum planning, are sufficiently high to extend the previous knowledge, skills and understanding of all pupils in a range of lessons and activities over time*
- *teaching enables pupils to develop skills in reading, writing, communication and mathematics*
- *teaching strategies, including setting challenging tasks matched to pupils' learning needs, successfully engage all pupils in their learning*
- *teachers secure high quality learning by setting challenging tasks that are matched to pupils' specific learning needs*
- *pupils understand how to improve their learning as a result of frequent, detailed and accurate feedback from teachers*
- *questioning and use of discussion promote learning*
- *the pace and depth of learning are maximised*
- *teachers enthuse, engage and motivate pupils to learn and foster their curiosity and enthusiasm for learning*
- *teachers use their expertise, including their subject knowledge, to develop pupils' knowledge, skills and understanding across a range of subjects and areas of learning*
- *teachers enable pupils to develop the skills to learn for themselves, where appropriate, including setting appropriate homework to develop their understanding* (OfSTED, 2012, p.15).

Inspectors will regard learning as effective if:

- *pupils develop a range of skills, including reading, writing, communication and mathematical skills, and how well they apply these across the curriculum*

/continued

Critical thinking exercise 2 – continued

- *disabled pupils and those who have special educational needs have achieved since joining the school*
- *gaps are narrowing between the performance of different groups of pupils in the school and compared to all pupils nationally*
- *pupils make progress relative to their starting points.*

(OfSTED, 2012, p.14)

1 **Consider** what this list tells us about what OfSTED values as being effective teaching and learning.

2. Are there any aspects of teaching and learning listed above that you would **challenge** as not being of significant value?

3 **Explore** other aspects of teaching and learning that are not on this list but still might be considered as being of value.

Comment

While using OfSTED criteria for making decisions about values and ethics in education is contentious it can be a useful starting point, as the OfSTED frameworks for inspection provide a public view and a benchmark for what is expected from education and schools. Indeed, OfSTED does not tell schools how they should be doing things, it is left to schools to make their own decisions about how to go about teaching and learning and OfSTED make judgements about how effective it believes the outcome of a school's teaching and learning is. So, as a minimum it would seem from the exercise above that we know that what OfSTED values in terms of teaching and learning is children making progress in learning; in particular, OfSTED cites progress in reading, writing, communication and mathematics. We can also see that OfSTED has an ethical view about how this should be happening. OfSTED wants all children, whatever their needs and background, to make progress; it wants learning to be exciting and motivating, and expects that teachers will have a good understanding of the subjects they are teaching and that children are supported in their learning. How does what OfSTED considers to be of value and an ethical approach match with your own beliefs in this area?

Key idea: **Behaviourism**

Exploring the behaviourist approach to teaching and learning

Behaviourists define learning as a relatively permanent change in behaviour as the result of experience (Jordan et al., 2008, p.21). In relation to education this would mean that in the classroom we would expect children to be developing or changing their skills, knowledge and understanding in response to the learning activities we design for them.

Classical behaviourist theory (Jordan et al., 2008) suggests that children can become conditioned to respond in a particular way to when a specific stimulus occurs. So, for example, this is often seen in relation to encouraging children to behave in a certain way, where we might constantly reward wanted behaviours and punish unwanted behaviours. There is some debate as to whether this approach to learning can have the same results in terms of cognitive learning. That is to say, behaviourism is linked to the notion that we know a change has taken place because behaviour changes, which is not always possible to determine in terms of 'seeing' changes in how a child thinks. However, it may be possible to infer changes in cognitive process through observing behaviours such as how a child can now make connections between ideas and concepts, or apply concepts in a way previously unobserved, for example through solving mathematics problems after being taught particular mathematics concepts. Some teachers challenge behaviourist theory because it does not help in discussing teaching and learning, since if we value the behaviourist approach we cannot know if the child can apply what he or she seems to have learnt because they have worked it out for themselves, or because they have learnt to approach a particular problem a certain way though being *conditioned* to do so in mathematics lessons. A further challenge to behaviourism is that it can seem to suggest that children are incapable of voluntary self-motivated behaviour and behave only in learnt ways as a response to the stimuli they have been conditioned by.

Key idea: **Constructivism**

The constructivist approach to teaching and learning

Brooks and Brooks (1999) describe constructivism as being the way in which *each of us makes sense of our world by synthesizing new experiences into what we have previously come to understand* (1999, p.4). In this way, learning is seen as being dynamic (Brooks and Brooks, 1999) and, to a certain extent, driven by itself rather than entirely by outside forces.

To illustrate the point above, consider, for example, moving to a new area. Initially we learn our way around the immediate environment we live in and, often with the use of maps, satellite navigation instruments, being shown, or trial and error, we find our way from our new home to the places we need to go to. Eventually we will come to build up a mental image – or cognitive map – of the wider area. We may even place this new knowledge of this previously unknown location in a wider map of the region, country or even of our cognitive map of the world. We construct what we know from the point at which we begin, we add to our understanding as our knowledge increases. In relation to learning about new places this means we find new routes of getting around the area, short cuts, shops and places to eat we prefer to the first ones we used. This is a more chaotic view of how learning might take place and note that sometimes we do get lost and go off in the wrong direction, but often it is learning that has more value to us because it is relevant and meaningful.

Critical thinking exercise 3

The following extract from OfSTED's report *Early years: getting on well: Enjoying, achieving and contributing* documents examples of what is seen as good practice in terms of children's learning activities.

> *Children enjoy stories and rhymes, which are often lively and interactive, and develop a love of favourite books. Children can be seen modelling storytelling and good book behaviour to one another as they use the book area to share stories and play 'schools'. Children achieve very well in this area; some enjoy making up and dramatising their own stories to a delighted audience of friends and teachers. Children like to make scrapbooks to record things they have done, using pictures and words. Children used porridge oats with the weighing scales ... children often record their findings on charts or simple graphs, giving a visual dimension to their understanding of quite abstract concepts.*

(OfSTED, 2007, p.13)

1 **Articulate** how the activities reported here are all relevant to children's day-to-day experiences.

2 **Analyse** the number of different curriculum subjects children are engaged with. That is, what are the children learning?

3 **Explore** what you think may be of value in approaching learning in this way.

Comment

You may find that you value aspects of both the learning theories explored above. It is important to give these theories some thought, as what you value about how children learn will impact on the ethics of how you go about teaching. For example, if you believe children are conditioned to learn through particular stimuli you may approach your teaching with a different ethical underpinning to those who value the notion that children construct meaning through being provided with a range of learning experiences and learning environments. The next few sections of this chapter explore ways of approaching teaching, learning and managing behaviour for learning through the values of behaviourism and constructivism.

Key idea: **Play**

Why is play an important part of teaching and learning?

Many educationalists place considerable emphasis on play having value in positively supporting teaching and learning in the classroom. A play-based approach to teaching and learning is also in line with OfSTED's notion of teaching and learning being enjoyable and therefore motivating (see above). However, others have ethical concerns that play is not conducive to teaching and learning, therefore it is important to discuss the purpose of play in the classroom.

In examining how teaching and learning through play offers children a better educational opportunity, there are many theorists who support this approach. Amongst them, Dewey argued that *experiential learning,* where children manipulate objects and situations, is more effective than a focus on content (Dewey, 1916[1966]). Play-based teaching and learning gives children a context within which they can situate new information and concepts, and helps to keep children's intellect engaged and progressing (Dewey 1916[1966], p.234). It has also been noted that play can reduce stress in children, enabling them to focus and identify goals in their learning experience and therefore enhance attainment. If children can actively reflect upon their play, through for example a 'Plan–Do–Review' approach, they can begin to analyse their own as well as other children's actions and incidents, making play meaningful in supporting the development of ethics and values.

However, it is not, as Dewey contends, enough just to introduce play, it is also dependent upon the way in which it is employed (1966). As discussed by Moyles (2005), *play and learning are inextricably linked* (2005, p.10) and when play activities are appropriately constructed they can support children's learning (p.10) across the whole curriculum and not just in the early years.

Key idea: **Assessing learning**

How can learning through play be properly assessed?

A concern with a play-based curriculum may be in knowing whether learning has actually occurred. Assessing children through play would seem like an impossible endeavour. When children play, no physical product seems to be created, marks or levels cannot be assigned and so differentiation between each child's achievements seems challenging. As with all learning activities, however, including play-based activities, you will construct the activity to meet particular learning outcomes you have identified. In determining whether a child has achieved the learning you intended you could observe and note what they are doing – or ask a teaching assistant to do this. You could talk to the child afterwards and ask questions to determine what they have learnt.

The Early Years Foundation Stage Curriculum is almost entirely 'play-based' and the guidance *advocates play and exploration as a basis for literacy learning in the early years* and *emphasises the importance of developing literacy through play* (DCSF, 2008a). This may prompt us to question why the Foundation Stage is primarily play-orientated and KS1 and 2 can seem to have almost no teaching or learning through play. Further to this, it can seem an arbitrary decision to stop play-based learning in Year 1, particularly if we consider Dewey's and other theorists' views as being of importance. There is a suggestion that moving to a more formal approach to teaching and learning can account for why some children experience discontinuity (Brooker, 2008, p.76) in their learning, particularly from YR to Y1. As Gardner (1991) argued, all pupils do not learn in the same way, and formal learning methods that do not meet the learning style of the child may exacerbate this discontinuity. As shown above, a play approach to teaching and learning is often more associated with young children rather than those in KS1 and 2. However, many schools adopt an experiential approach to teaching and learning which does provide children with the opportunities to learn through an interactive, often play-based approach.

Key idea: **Creativity**

How teaching through creativity can promote learning

In practice, many schools use a range of teaching and learning approaches to engage children in their learning. This section explores the value of creativity in the curriculum. Creativity is often associated with the 'creative arts' but in reality it is certainly not unique to the arts. It can be seen and identified in all aspects of the arts, humanities, sciences, mathematics and technology. *The National Curriculum Handbook* (DfEE and QCA, 1999) included creativity within the section on thinking skills, stating that: *Creative thinking skills ... enable pupils to generate and extend ideas, to suggest hypotheses, to apply imagination and to look for alternative innovative outcomes.* The Early Learning Goals within the Foundation Stage Curriculum Guidance also state that creativity is fundamental to successful learning, and the EYFS states: *children's creativity must be extended by the provision of support for their curiosity, exploration and play* (DCSF, 2008a).

If, as Craft (2000) describes, creativity is *a state of mind in which all our intelligences are working together... [involving] seeing, thinking and innovating* (p.38), then a more creative learning experience would more enable our children to tackle complexity and be adaptable in the face of our ever-changing global environment. Governments worldwide are now more concerned than ever to promote creativity because creativity can lead to new inventions, concepts and so on, which have economic importance.

The UK saw an initial drive towards a more creative curriculum over ten years ago with the publication of *All our futures: Creativity, culture and education* (NACCCE, 1999). Moreover, the government Creative Partnership initiative (OfSTED, 2002a) aimed to

---

give young people in disadvantaged areas across England the opportunity to develop their creativity and ambition by building partnerships between schools and creative organisations, businesses and individuals. More recently, OfSTED's (2010b) report *Learning: creative approaches that raise standards* noted:

> *pupils who were supported by good teaching that encouraged questioning, debate, experimentation, presentation and critical reflection enjoyed the challenge and had a sense of personal achievement. The confidence they gained encouraged them to develop and present their own ideas with greater imagination and fluency.*

(OfSTED, 2010b, p.5).

The process of teaching creatively is an interpersonal journey that is far more nuanced and complex than simply a teacher's mastery of curricula and pedagogical techniques. This process embodies the ethical and value-based nature of a teacher's professionalism which is often overshadowed by accountability or practical aspects of teaching and learning. Whilst we cannot dismiss these responsibilities and aspects we should consider that education in its broadest sense is about the development and formation of children as persons. It necessitates us to view what is valuable and what constitutes a 'developed person'. One central characteristic of such a person is their capacity to live within and to contribute to the community. A global, ethical dimension therefore becomes imperative and integral rather than peripheral if the underlying values are seen as part of the learning process.

Nevertheless, the implementation of creativity often faces barriers within schools as it can be considered of lesser importance or 'unobtainable'. Some schools overloaded with the National Curriculum and immersed in a culture of accountability with the continuing pressures of OfSTED inspections, league tables, and sometimes a lack of teacher confidence and insecure subject knowledge can inevitably lead to a more didactic approach. Such external pressures can limit opportunities for creative endeavour and may result in many teachers 'playing safe' by offering a curriculum largely dictated and developed by others, such as the QCA, rather than one developed in response to children's needs, interests and the cultural capital within the school and community.

Sternberg (1999) suggests creative teachers are creative role models themselves; such professionals continue to be self-motivated learners, who value the creative dimensions of their own lives and make connections between their personal responses to experience and their teaching. These creative teachers tend to be more learner-centred and value the learning experience over curriculum. Values such as openness, respect, support and trust whereby the individual is accepted, valued and ideas are discussed and celebrated are embedded in this creative teaching. As Halpin (2003) notes: *pupils [should be able to] feel confident enough to take risks and learn from failure instead of being branded by it. ... they should react positively to self help questions like; 'Am I safe here?' 'Do I belong?' 'Can I count on others to support me?'* (cited in Grainger and Barnes, 2006, p.7).

One of the values of play and creative approaches to teaching and learning is that all learners can be fully engaged through appealing to their own interests and passions, by involving them in imaginative experiences, and by connecting their learning to their lives (Grainger and Barnes, 2006) as well as 'transmitting knowledge' as perhaps required by aspects of the National Curriculum. While it may be more difficult to measure the success of a creative approach to primary learning and teaching, a more creative learning experience will equip children with adaptable and transferable life skills they will need in the rapidly changing world and work environments of the future. Clearly a more creative curriculum, driven by the values identified above and the core ethical beliefs explored, would be a more interdisciplinary approach and one that brings knowledge into a context rather than delivering knowledge for its own sake.

Critical thinking exercise 4

To what extent have you observed children taking ownership of their own learning? Do they make decisions, discuss options and ideas openly?

To what extent was the work matched to the needs and interests of the children? Were they emotionally or imaginatively engaged?

To what extent were they able to express their individuality and also work collaboratively? Are they able to take risks?

If you have seen little evidence of these issues, consider how you could offer more opportunity for ownership, relevance and individuality in the classroom.

1 **Consider** your current tutors or previous teachers. Which are/were the most creative teachers? How did they create successful learning experiences in which you felt valued and engaged, to take risks, make connections and develop deep learning? How do/did they achieve this?

2 **Articulate** what your reflection tells you about how you currently perceive creative teachers.

3 **Analyse** if there is a tendency to assume creative teachers are extrovert, effervescent professionals, instead of focusing on the creative learning experience facilitated.

Comment

For a school's teaching and learning approach to be successful in ensuring that effective learning is happening it is necessary for there to be an agreed approach to core values, such as valuing children's voice, and involvement and ownership of both the school environment and the curriculum, which can integrate these values into the very fibre of the school. All teaching and learning approaches, including those based on the ethics of play approaches and creativity, need to be agreed not only by teaching staff, but by the whole school and its community too. Successful teaching and learning happens when all involved in the process understand what is being valued and the ethics that underpin how the teaching and learning is being approached.

Key idea: **The learning environment**

How you organise your classroom will impact on teaching and learning

Just as the way we approach teaching and learning will impact on what happens in our classrooms, so too will the way we organise our classroom environment. How classrooms are organised reflects what we value about teaching and learning and the ethics of how we go about teaching children and enabling children to learn. The school and classroom environment can have a significant influence on a child. There are a myriad of considerations when preparing and maintaining the 'right' classroom environment, particularly one that enriches learning. Some consider that quality space can stimulate the brain and in turn optimise a child's performance and so when designing a classroom space we need to value how the classroom feels for both the adults and children within it.

Critical thinking exercise 5

Draw an outline of a classroom – draw in some rectangles to represent tables or areas children might sit down and work at. Then mark 30 'dots' to represent children. Now plan a classroom designed to promote your ethics and values. Reflect upon some of these issues:

- *Where will resources be stored?*
- *How are you going to group the tables for maximum flexibility – or do you want a fixed arrangement?*
- *Will you need a teacher's desk?*
- *How can you make fullest use of the door to the playground and outdoor learning?*
- *How are you going to create themed or focused interest and activity areas?*
- *Will you have a role-play area in the classroom?*

/continued

Critical thinking exercise 5 – continued

- *How are the display spaces going to be used? What will they display?*
- *How can you cater for the diversity of needs within the class? Consider a child who likes to work alone and the access needs of a child in a wheelchair.*
- *Are you expecting children will have some independence and autonomy in how the classroom is arranged and in moving round the room to get the things they need – or to move to particular activity areas as necessary?*
- *Where will the whiteboard and computers be?*

1 **Imagine** different configurations.

2 **Explore** the range of possibilities.

3 **Analyse** what your preferred solution says about your values and ethics with regard to your classroom as a learning environment.

Comment

How you organise your classroom will reflect your values in terms of your approach to children and teaching and learning. How you have arranged the tables, allowed routes around the room, provided for collaborative working areas, books to be read, visibility of the whiteboard, interactive displays and space for pupil interaction and access to the outside environment, for example, will say something about your values and the ethics that underpin your teaching and learning approaches. That is, you may have arranged things to allow for play-based and creative approaches where children are active in the learning process or you may have decided on a more formal approach to organising your classroom. However you have decided to manage your learning environment, engagement with this chapter should provide you with the theoretical underpinning to defend your ethics and values with regard to your approach to teaching and learning.

Key ideas: **Managing behaviour**

How do we teach children to behave well?

Behaviour is often regarded as an area of concern and indeed stress for many trainee and qualified teachers. The recent government White Paper *The Importance of Teaching* (DfE, 2010) identifies a shift in definition from 'behaviour management' to 'discipline'. If we were to list five actions or attitudes for either term our lists may be quite different and so we may find our core values and beliefs are either complemented or in conflict. Discipline may evoke past images of corporal

/continued

Key ideas: **Managing behaviour** – continued

punishment and words such as training, compliance and consequence associated with it. Behaviour management may focus us upon words such as modification, strategies, rewards, contracts and evoke images of a collaborative approach. If we discuss with others what they believe good behaviour and bad behaviour to look like, we might also find that there are many different understandings of these terms. However, research does show that a strong aspect of successful behaviour management is that schools need to have an agreed and consistent approach to encouraging good behaviour and dealing with unwanted behaviour. In addition, they need to ensure their teaching and learning approaches are motivating and interesting.

The recent Department for Education paper *Ensuring good behaviour in schools: A summary for headteachers, governing bodies, teachers, parents and pupils* (DfE, 2011b) states that, in terms of defining behaviours that are valued, the government expects *all pupils to show respect and courtesy towards teachers and other staff and towards each other* (DfE, 2011b, p.1). To ensure this sort of behaviour is happening, the same document states that disciplining children to behave is the responsibility of schools and that parents too have an ethical imperative *to encourage their children to show that respect and support the school's authority to discipline its pupils* (p.1). While these comments do not necessarily seem contentious in themselves, in that many value respect and courtesy, what may be more contentious is how the ethics of teaching these values and demonstrating these values may be interpreted quite differently by different people. As such, take a moment to engage with the activity below to illustrate this.

CASE STUDY

A teacher within a school you are working in is known to rarely say please and thank you, is often abrupt with both children and adults, and rarely explains their actions. You are helping a group in this class with making a collage for display. A child snatches the last glue stick from you and two others complain, the child tells them to *shut up*. You reprimand the child and insist she shows some manners and respect. She responds, *Well, Mr Smith never says please and thank you and never says we should . . . and he told us all to shut up this morning.*

A **Articulate** what you would do in this situation.

B **Analyse** how your role as an adult modelling behaviour in a classroom impacts on the values you communicate to children.

C **Compare** how different responses to the situation will affect the children.

Comment

If you say Mr Smith is wrong you are undermining his authority, but if you do not address this issue you may be in conflict with your own core values. The way you choose to resolve this situation will indicate much about your own values and ethics with regard to managing behaviour. Many people would consider the simple use of please and thank you as a first when being courteous.

Regardless of the terms, both behaviour management and discipline should be underpinned by a clear philosophy of behaviour for learning, as learning is at the heart of education. If we are meeting the needs of all learners, often undesirable behaviours will diminish. Sir Alan Steer's (2009) report on behaviour in schools concluded that:

> *consistent good quality teaching is the most significant factor in raising standards and reducing low level disruption [para 54] ... The link between teaching quality and pupil behaviour is most evident in the skill with which the teacher uses the <u>curriculum</u> to hold children's attention in the first place. A child who is absorbed in learning is less likely to become disengaged – and to misbehave in consequence.*

(Steer, 2009, para 4.16)

The major source of conflict or concern may be with the consideration of the *summmum bonum*, the greatest good, coupled with the government expectation *that every teacher will be good at managing and improving children's behaviour*. (DfE, 2011b, p.1).

A teacher is expected to manage the whole class, with the diverse range of individuals within it. A starting point is often to create a *whole class vision*. The class envisages what would happen in their ideal classroom, such as working collaboratively, listening to each other or being more considerate. This should complement the school ethos and bring a direct correlation between values and behaviour. However, many schools and teachers may talk about values once a month or once a week, often in assemblies, and fail to integrate them into the culture as a whole. This approach, although 'ticking the ethics and values box' fails to take advantage of the opportunity to teach ethics by role modelling and through the power of the 'hidden curriculum'. Children will identify with actions and attitudes more quickly and with a greater impact than any words could communicate. Moreover, it will also result in implying, at worst, that such core principles only matter on Monday morning at 9.00 a.m., or that particular value is only important for that week.

Therefore we must model our values, and repetition and reinforcement are key to this. The introduction of a value-based vocabulary can encourage more reflective thinking, which can lead to more positive and ethically based behaviour. Also, using this vocabulary during regular discussion about values reinforces their meaning, with the result that they are more likely to be embedded more fully.

Many view the role of teachers as one that is inherently moral and ethical, and as discussed in Chapter 1, teachers directly influence children. There is also a need, however, to recognise that there are tensions and challenges that have the potential to lead to what may be perceived as *morally objectionable* situations leading to *ethically questionable* behaviour from those working in that environment. Moral conflicts may occur among teachers and those adults working with the children, as well as between teachers, children, headteachers, governors, parents or the local authority and also within individual teachers themselves. Teachers may struggle to do what they may think is the 'right thing' as they may have to deal with controversial issues, and so need the awareness and skills to handle controversy.

Critical thinking exercise 6

Reflect upon these possible scenarios:

1) It is the end of the school day and you see a fight in the playground between two children. You know that if you contact the parents of one of them the child will be punished at home and may be very withdrawn and tearful the next day.
2) You 'catch' a child taking a box of pencils and paper. You know this child does not have pencils and paper at home.

A **Articulate** what preconceptions you may have of the children and parents that may affect your course of action.

B **Reflect** if your knowledge of home life affects your judgement.

C **Consider** its effect on your own moral and ethical code.

Comment

The dilemmas here are addressing preconceptions, taking the right action adhering to the school's policy, as well as acknowledging outcomes that will affect both children. As teachers we need to make practical decisions where there may be no clear answer; to make judgements in the light of the facts gathered and recognise that our decisions may need to be affected in light of further evidence; to be open to criticism and accepting of the 'voice' of others, especially our children and parents. We have to know our own ethical responsibility and core values so that decisions made are based upon fact and irrefutable principles.

Children will behave if motivated and interested in the tasks they are doing. Make sure each child has a task that they can do, but challenges them and moves them on in their learning – make sure the way you are asking the child to complete the task is purposeful – not just the 'same old' writing. Recall what you found or find motivating when learning and how you may apply this to your teaching.

Constantly reward the behaviours you want – either with verbal praise or by giving out stickers, or through a class reward system:

> We've worked so hard – especially Said's table; let's have 5 minutes extra break.

> Well done Zane, you have got the idea – everybody, can you just have a look at this . . .

> That's it, Sarah, you have thought about . . .

Go back to your discussion about children's voice – if they feel part of the process, they will behave.

 Teachers, teaching assistants and other paid staff with responsibility for pupils have the power to discipline pupils whose behaviour is unacceptable, who break the school rules or who fail to follow a reasonable instruction. Their power to discipline applies to pupil behaviour in school and outside school, in certain circumstances.

(DfE, 2011b, p.2)

Critical thinking exercise 7

Despite the 'catch 'em being good' approach and emphasis on praise and reward, some children some of the time will need punishment and a hierarchy of sanctions is used by many schools. This hierarchy must be matched to the 'level' of unacceptable behaviour.

Consider applying three levels – low, medium and high – to categorise and decide upon the sanction. Match these possible behaviours below to a level:

1) A child is mumbling under their breath.
2) A child throws a rubber across the room.
3) A child grabs another child's work and rips it.
4) A child shouts out and others respond laughing.
5) A child refuses to comply with your instruction and sits doing no work.
6) A child picks up a chair with intent to throw it.
7) A child physically grabs another child and threatens them.

1 **Consider** the values that underpin the rules these children may have broken. Do some rules we have for behaviour have more value than others?

2 **Articulate** what might be suitable punishments for breaking these rules.

3 **Analyse** why you are responding in the way you are – who has taught you to respond in this way?

Comment

Your response and sanction affects the individual child and the whole class. Should you stop and affect the learning of the whole class in addressing scenario 1 or punish the whole class for scenario 4? When addressing scenarios 6 and 7 the school should consider *whether the behaviour under review gives cause to suspect that a child is suffering, or is likely to suffer, significant harm. Where this may be the case, school staff should follow the schools' safeguarding policy. They should also consider whether continuing disruptive behaviour might be the result of unmet educational or other needs. At this point, the school should consider whether a multi-agency assessment is necessary* (DfE, 2011a, pp.4–5).

As set out in the DfE's (2011a) *Behaviour and discipline in schools: A guide for headteachers and school staff*, to be lawful a punishment, which includes detentions, must satisfy three conditions:

1. *The decision to punish a pupil must be made by a paid member of school staff or a member of staff authorised by the headteacher;*

2. *The decision to punish the pupil and the punishment itself must be made on the school premises or while the pupil is under the charge of the member of staff; and*

3. *It must not breach any other legislation (for example in respect of disability, Special Educational Needs, race and other equalities and human rights) and it must be reasonable in all the circumstances.*

(DfE, 2011a, p.4)

Perhaps the best guidance in terms of knowing how to approach behaviour management, particularly as a new member of staff in a school, is to work through the items on the list below:

1. Read the school's behaviour management policy.
2. Talk it over with the headteacher, or a senior member of staff. Ask them, if X happened, could I do Y? Or should I do Z?
3. Observe how the senior members of staff show through their leadership what they expect in terms of behaviour and how they manage behaviour – you could ask to observe a particular teacher for a day or two.
4. Look for consistency in the way staff manage behaviour, that is, all the staff work to the same rules, rewards and punishments. Consistency enables the children to know what the rules are as it means they are the same everywhere.
5. Find out how the school rewards good behaviour and punishes bad behaviour.
6. Think through your own views on what you regard as low-level disruption and very poor behaviour.
7. Consider the messages you are giving in the way you behave towards the children and other adults in the school.

Conclusion

What teaching styles to adopt, how to construct motivating and interesting learning activities as well as managing behaviour are aspects of education that often most concern those working in schools. Thinking through the fundamental values and ethics you hold with regard to these aspects of education will help strengthen all aspects of your professional skills. For these reasons this chapter has:

- explored different approaches to teaching, learning and managing behaviour;
- asked you to anlayse what you feel is important to you about the ideas discussed; and
- encouraged you to consider how what you have read might be used to develop your professional skills and classroom practice.

Further Reading

Arthur, J, Grainger, T and Wray, D (eds) (2006) *Learning to teach in the primary school.* London: Routledge.

DfE (2011) *Ensuring good behaviour in schools: A summary for head teachers, governing bodies, teachers, parents and pupils.* London: DfE.

Jordan, A Carlile, O and Stack, A (2008) *Approaches to learning: A guide for teachers.* Maidenheads: Open University Press.

7 Children and young people

Linda Cooper

Chapter Focus

The critical thinking exercises in this chapter focus on:

⊙ **analysing** the underlying principles of the issues being discussed;
⊙ **articulating** what underpins your own approach to the issues being discussed;
⊙ **comparing** a range of approaches and outcomes;
⊙ **considering** what ideas provide the most helpful way forward to resolving conflicting situations;
⊙ **discussing** the tensions between competing ideas;
⊙ **exploring** how issues can be approached in different ways;
⊙ **imagining** different approaches to a situation.

The key ideas discussed are: **Dewey and the holistic view of education, perceptions of childhood, children's voice, the development of responsible adults, the voice of the child, school councils, circle time, involving children in target-setting and assessment** and **international comparisons.**

This chapter is particularly relevant to Teachers' Standards: **1, 4, 5, 6, 7** and **8**.

Introduction

As we have explored throughout this book, the role of 'education' in a primary school can be defined in numerous different ways. Examined from a very narrow viewpoint, the education a school might provide could be seen as one where children learn the mechanisms of reading, writing and arithmetic. It could be argued that it is about fostering subject knowledge and the development of conceptual understanding, while the responsibility for nurturing the wider personality of the child would be left to the parent and the home environment. If this view of schooling and education was accurate we might expect education to be without contention and teaching to be a simple matter. However, education is neither non-controversial nor straightforward, reflecting the long-acknowledged fact that schools have a more complex function in society.

Key idea: **Educating the whole child**

Dewey and what we mean by an holistic education

In 1897 John Dewey outlined his view that education involved much more than the transmission of knowledge and ought to give the child command of himself and the full and ready use of all his capacities (Dewey, 1897, px). He concluded that: *education is a regulation of the process of coming to share in the social consciousness; and that the adjustment of individual activity on the basis of this social consciousness is the only sure method of social reconstruction* (Dewey, 1897).

From this perspective, the role of the school is not limited to helping individual children acquire knowledge, it has a much wider and more profound influence; it sustains and potentially transforms society. From the time of Dewey, the complex role of education has continued to develop. The prospective educator has only to view some of the central statutory documents that are used in school to understand this, and these provide a good place to start exploring the 'role of education'.

Critical thinking exercise 1

At the beginning of the National Curriculum published in 1999 (DFEE and QCA, 1999) it is stated that one of the aims of educating children through this curriculum is: *The school curriculum should aim to promote pupils' spiritual, moral, social and cultural development and prepare all pupils for the opportunities, responsibilities and experiences of life'* (DFEE & QCA, 1999, p.11).

When expanding on this aim, it is stated that: *The school curriculum should pass on enduring values, develop pupils' integrity and autonomy and help them to be responsible citizens capable of contributing to the development of a just society* (p.11).

1   **Analyse** how you as a practitioner prepare the children you work with to meet this aim.

2   **Consider** in the current review of this curriculum if you would want this to be an aim you would wish to keep for the children in your school, or would you want it taken out of the new curriculum aims?

3   **Discuss** with others the importance of having values such as the ones detailed above in statutory documents. Should they be decided by government or within the community of the school itself?

Comment

The aims of the 1999 National Curriculum (DFEE & QCA, 1999) show that the teaching profession is informed by a values-driven document. The aim listed above demonstrates a commitment to a remit that goes beyond the scope of the narrow view that education is purely about the transmission of knowledge. The 'principles' and 'commitments' of the Early Years Foundation Stage Curriculum (DCSF, 2008a) also adhere to the broader role of education and emphasise the importance of nurturing the personality of the child. Commitments that advocate the enabling of young children to *discover boundaries, make choices, understand feelings* and *respect diversity* indicate that this is a document that attributes schools with an holistic developmental role (DCSF, 2008b). It is as committed to the overall welfare of the child as it is to the acquisition of basic knowledge and skills.

Apart from curriculum documents, there are other key agendas that have had an influence on the course of educational developments in the UK. Some of these deserve exploration in the context of this discussion, particularly the United Nations Convention on the Rights of the Child (UNCRC), which was ratified by the UK government in 1991. This document contains 40 'human rights' – promises undertaken by signatory governments to treat people equally and fairly (NICCY, 2009) – which are deemed to apply to all individuals below the age of 18 (UNICEF, 2006). While it is not the remit of this chapter to examine each of the 'promises' made to children in the UNCRC, one area of the document is of particular importance. As Roche et al. (2004) suggest, the most vital part of this treaty centres on a concern with what is coined the 'three Ps': provision of services, protection and participation. It is the theme of 'participation' of children that needs further analysis in this discussion. Article 12 of the UNCRC deserves explicit attention; it states that:

 Parties shall assure to the child who is capable of forming his or her own views the right to express those views freely in all matters affecting the child, the views of the child being given due weight in accordance with the age and maturity of the child.

(Office of the United Nations High Commissioner for Human Rights, 2009)

Though this treaty is not ratified by law, it is an important step in defining children as active participants in society and influences how children should be viewed. If this participation really is to occur, then education has a major role in the fulfilment of this right.

Another significant document, one that does have legal force, is the Children Act of 2004, which contributes to the same discourse on the participation of the child in school. The resulting agenda of Every Child Matters, which was a direct outcome of the Act, produced the now well-known central themes of: *be healthy; stay safe; enjoy and achieve; make a positive contribution;* and *achieve economic wellbeing* (DfES, 2004). It is the areas of 'enjoyment and achievement' and that of 'making a positive contribution' that need further discussion in this chapter and will be returned to in future paragraphs. However, it is worth pausing here to re-emphasise the multifaceted nature of education and to consolidate the points made so far.

Those studying education and training to be teachers do not need to spend long on their programme to realise the complex challenge of education. As we have seen in Chapter 4, students on any good education programme will quickly be confronted with the fact that education is about much more than the simple transmission of knowledge. They will understand that they have to equip the children they work with with a range of transferable skills that can be used throughout the school career and will prove just as valuable as subject knowledge. For instance, they will come to understand that the subjects they teach to children involve more than delivery of facts but also require children to understand concepts and processes that arise within the context of individual subjects, but can be applied more widely. They will also realise that the acquisition of 'tools for learning', like the ability to problem-solve or evaluate information, is just as important as the development of operations like being able to divide numbers or naming the different monarchs of the Tudor period.

In addition to this, and perhaps most importantly, the above curriculum documents and agendas show that those involved in the job of nurturing children are doing so in order that they become active participants in society and citizens of the future. However, this already significant challenge is made harder by a climate that creates a focus on standards and demonstrating improvements in test results. 'Achievement' in this context is measured by progression through attainment targets and results in national tests (Woolley, 2008), which can be seen to promote an emphasis on the transmission of knowledge and conceptual understanding. The supposed 'success' of a child is obtained by their association with the dominant curriculum subjects of literacy and numeracy. The importance of being literate and numerate cannot be denied, but the increasingly narrow curriculum, which is allied to the focus on testing in the primary school, does mean that some children are more likely to experience failure at an early age. Of course, as an educationalist and a parent, I want my own children to be competent in literacy and efficient in their arithmetic calculations. However, I also hold other aspirations for them. I would like them to be active participants in their class, independent learners, mature and resilient human beings who take responsibility for their own progress. These issues are as important to me as their success in literacy and numeracy when I read a report.

At the same time, other trends within the wider educational environment, particularly an increasingly prescriptive approach to not only what to teach, but how to teach it, threaten to stifle potential progress in promoting children's participation in their learning (Sinclair Taylor, 2000). The focus on whole-class teaching, for example, which was a feature of previous literacy and numeracy strategies, is described as a disenfranchising methodology, which opposes a child-centred approach in favour of subject mastery. Sinclair Taylor likens this to an *authoritarian and didactic approach* (2000, p.30).

Critical thinking exercise 2

As a result of the Children Act 2004, the Every Child Matters (ECM) agenda was introduced into Early Years settings and schools. The ECM agenda requires those who work with children ensure children are enabled to achieve the five outcomes of: being mentally, physically and emotionally healthy; being safe; enjoying and achieving in their learning; contributing to the society they belong to; and going on to achieve economic wellbeing.

Look around your current work place or recall a school you have spent time in. Look on the walls and in public spaces like reception areas. Emblems and badges like 'Healthy School Marks' are part of the Every Child Matters agenda. Look and list just how many other influences can be attributed to the ECM framework.

1 **Analyse** how these five outcomes influence every part of a child's life, both in the short and long term.

2 **Consider** how such outcomes as being safe and being healthy relate to the learning aspect of education.

3 **Articulate** an example of good practice you have seen that supports the achievement of one of these outcomes.

Comment

It was concern about the increasingly prescriptive, test-saturated curriculum, standardisation and a one-size fits all approach that led to creation of documents like Every Child Matters (2004). This initiative refreshed the ideal of recognising the unique nature of each child as an individual. Themes like 'making a positive contribution' led to a renewed importance of listening to the child, participation of all groups of children and an emphasis on hearing the child's voice. More recently the additional theme of 'personalisation', the tailoring of each child's learning experience, has gained momentum in the primary classroom. The emergence of this agenda was also a response to an increasingly urgent appeal to take action on the state of childhood in the UK. When this document first appeared there was concern that 'childhood' was a pressured state and certain conditions were combining to give children poor starts in life. It is at this point that it might be worthwhile pausing to briefly explore current perceptions of the condition of the child in the UK.

Key ideas: **Childhood**

What do we mean when we use the term childhood?

The period of early childhood (i.e. those years before adolescence) has traditionally been seen as a time of innocence, during which children should be sheltered and protected. This time is also associated with perceptions of 'freedom' in a sense that children do not have any responsibility and should also have the liberty and the space to play. However, more recently this 'ideal' of the young child has been perceived to be at risk from a variety of threats seen to be inherent in modern life, such as: overconcern with standards and achievement in education with, conversely, public anxiety about boys underachievement in schools; the potential risks posed through unregulated contact with others via the internet; the early sexualisation of girls by the media and retail industry; and concern about a perceived breakdown in traditional family life. Consequently, Wyness (2006) suggests there is now the notion that the late-modern construction of childhood is one of childhood as having become dominated by worry and anxiety and the need for moral rescue (Wyness, 2006).

Wyness (2006, p.75) goes on to argue that one of the dominant themes in contemporary Western society is childhood in crisis. The reasons for this supposed disintegration of the state of childhood are complex. Some of the key issues in this debate, however, will be outlined in the following few paragraphs.

Wyness (2006) states that parents are now trying to recapture the halcyon days of the childhood of the past, where they themselves were more carefree than their own children are today. Perhaps the most significant concern held by parents is that their children are not physically safe. Certainly this is a sentiment not to be sneered at, but it could be argued that society is very anxious (perhaps over-anxious) about several themes. There is concern that children cannot play outside due to the amount of road traffic and associated pollution risks, for example. The worry about outside play is compounded by the risk to the child from people who seek to do them harm. Several cases widely reported in the media, where children have been fatally harmed, like the murder of James Bulger in 1993, have led to extreme reactions on the part of some parents, who have gone to great lengths to keep their children safe. While this is both understandable and laudable, an exaggerated perception of the risks presented by these dangers can lead to responses that are out of proportion and potentially harmful in themselves. Wyness (2006, p.54) points to the state where generalised and non-specific feelings of anxiety are projected onto children and result in an overall tightening of parental control. Children, it might be argued, are increasingly under adult supervision and rarely get adequate opportunity to find their own confidence to cope in situations where their parents are not present.

These threats to the young child are accompanied by several other combining factors, including lack of sleep, excessive consumerism, social change and a lack of interaction in the home. This combined with an overprescriptive and test-driven curriculum has led to what has been termed as a *toxic childhood* (Palmer, 2006). Two other major factors in this 'toxic childhood syndrome' have yet to be mentioned – they are the influence of technology and the consequences of family breakdown.

Anecdotal evidence suggests that parents are broadly concerned about intrusion of technology into the lives of children. Stand with parents on any playground in the UK and you are likely to come across conversations in which concerns are expressed about the amount of time children spend watching television or using computers. The leisure pursuits of children have changed and it is not uncommon for them to spend several hours in the day involved in screen-based activities of this sort. Technology now constitutes an important feature in the social landscape of children; indeed Prensky (2001) has coined the term *digital native* for the child of the 21st century, capturing the notion of a generation who are both familiar with and immersed in technology. What is more, this threat has an additional dimension, as many adults find themselves in a situation where their offspring are more sophisticated technology users than they are. As a consequence, parents cannot relate to the experience of the child and therefore they cannot be 'in control' of them while they use it. This lack of control, heightened by the fact that virtual threats – such as paedophiles using social media – are 'unseen', makes technology feel extremely daunting.

Perceived family breakdown also constitutes a threat to the popular model of the ideal childhood. The effects of divorce on a child present a plethora of possible poor consequences, including negative impacts upon academic performance and general behavioural problems. It is suggested that children experiencing family breakdown suffer problems with self-esteem and form weaker social relationships (Palmer, 2006). Furthermore, children of divorced parents might also suffer the financial implications of living with a lone parent on only one income. The issues outlined above do detail some very disturbing scenarios that cannot be ignored. Children who are disaffected, impulsive, uninterested and poorly behaved do present a problem for school, parents, society and for the child's own personal prospects. However, in many of these situations it is tempting to paint children as helpless and powerless and to see them as victims of greater and overpowering societal changes. This, one might argue, leads to a false impression and one that is not constructive, as it contributes to generalisations that stigmatise children and marginalises them as individuals and actors in their own development.

This helpless and powerless state of the young child stands at the opposite end of the spectrum to the 'model' presented of children as they progress to adolescence. Here a different picture emerges. Where the young child is seen as a helpless victim, the adolescent youth is depicted as something to be feared. Knowles (2009) discusses this concept, suggesting that perceptions of this state of childhood constitute the *demonisation* of the child; a theme that emerged with particular force after the killing of Jamie Bulger, where the innocent child and the dangerous youth were juxtaposed in the popular imagination. There are also particular concerns about gangs of youths who roam streets uncontrolled and without boundaries on their behaviour; a picture that is often exacerbated by reports made in the media

Wyness (2006) discusses the problem of youth and states that the four points of delinquency, truancy, the demonisation of the child and the problem of teenage pregnancy are all themes that are associated with the weakening of the authority of parents over children. This argument can be related back to the previously discussed theme of the need to 'control' children. The issue of 'control', or the lack of it, when associated with the teenager is very current in the media. A short perusal of media listings will quickly reveal this as a dominant theme. There are TV programmes that claim to provide ways of taming unruly teenagers, programmes about 'unteachable' children, programmes following the lives of 'selfish' teenagers who live off their parents and numerous different productions that focus on teenage pregnancy.

It could be argued that if children are to succeed in becoming active participants and responsible citizens of the future, the images of them that are presented by the media need to change. Children do need to be kept safe from harm and there are 'problem teenagers', but depictions of young people also need to reflect the many children who are proactive, resilient, responsible decision-makers who make a contribution to the schools and communities in which they live.

Critical thinking exercise 3

Follow the news for a week and consider how the media are portraying children. Can you categorise the reports? Are children portrayed as helpless victims that need to be protected from society, or are they described as threatening youths that should be controlled? How many reports do you watch or read that portray children as responsible and proactive citizens of the future?

1 **Explore** how children are discussed in the media.

2 **Consider** what these images of children imply about how society views children.

3 **Articulate** your views on what you think it means to be a child.

Comment

While acknowledging that there has been anxiety over the state of childhood, especially for those who experience poverty, disadvantage, inequality or marginalisation, Alexander (2008) calls for an alternative assessment of childhood. He argues that his research found that while adults were indeed very worried about the condition of the child, children themselves actually presented a much more upbeat picture.

Key idea: **Children's voice**

What do we mean by the notion of children's voice?

Alexander advocates a shift from a viewpoint that presents children as *victims, problems or threats* to one that *celebrates what children can do as social beings* (2008, p.9). He argues that in fact it is often the parents who consider their offspring unhappy, not the children themselves. Put simply, Alexander embraces the theme of the empowerment of children and argues that to succeed with this *empowerment* children should be engaged with and listened to, not just talked at. He emphasises that one way to achieve this outcome is through practitioners valuing the importance of the child's voice.

Key idea: **School councils**

How do school councils give children a voice?

The most visible manifestation of the voice of the child in school is seen through the development of school councils, both at primary and secondary level. School councils are typically made up of a selection of nominated children from each year group of the school. The purpose of the council can vary from school to school, but usually it exists for children to be able to engage with issues associated with the school community. Councils provide a mechanism for children to express their views and to get involved in a range of issues, from small matters, like discussing school litter problems, to more important decisions, such as the appointment of a new teacher. Some school councils can have a financial dimension where children can influence decisions on how money is spent.

To ensure success, Taylor and Johnson (2002) state that the suggested aims of a council could include:

- *helping children to understand democratic procedures ... in order to aid the development of participative citizens in society;*

- *recognising a duty to respect children's rights;*

- *helping children to learn to care for each other;*

- *promoting better behaviour by giving children more responsibilities.*

(Taylor and Johnson, 2002, p.11).

Taylor and Johnson (2002) go on to argue that their own research on school councils demonstrated that the overall aim of this type of body was to give students a voice. Teachers claimed that a school council helped staff to see things from the point of view of the child and that they aided the development of a two-way process of communication. Furthermore, the council was said to help children feel valued and was responsible for the production of children who could discuss, debate and resolve issues (Taylor and Johnson, 2002).

School councils take time to establish, and for them to be successful entities they have to have the commitment of the school teaching staff behind them in order that they flourish and thrive in a busy school environment. It is also vital that an adult gives extra time to the process of the council business until it is fully integrated and recognised in the life of the school. In addition, for the process to work, children will need help in understanding how to carry out the business of a meeting in terms of keeping minutes and setting agendas. Indeed, if councils are to be 'democratic', children will need to explore how to present cases, negotiate and vote on issues at hand (Knowles, 2009).

School councils can certainly be seen as a positive development in the role of listening to children and helping them to develop as communicative, participative and active citizens of the future. Councils, however, are not without their problems. For these bodies to be effective it is vital that their impact and the work they are involved in is visible to the rest of the school community. Much work has to be undertaken with children to ensure that those on the council are representative and appointed through a democratic process. They should not become members of the body simply due to the fact that they are popular, for example. Primary school children might also take time to fully grasp the idea that it is not only their own wants and needs they are voicing on the council, but the thoughts and feelings of the class they represent. Meanwhile, it is important that when the council meeting is taking place that the younger, or less articulate members of the body, are not intimidated by older or more effusive peers. Moreover, in order that the views of the council do not become merely tokenistic, the staff body must be committed to listening to the deliberations and conclusions of the school council. The rest of the children in the school must also feel that they are somehow involved in this process and that information is passed to and from the council to the wider collective.

There is also the risk that schools that have produced a fully functioning council might conclude that they can feel satisfied that the child's voice is acknowledged in school. Councils are a good idea and provide one valid method of listening to children. However, even at their best, councils will only ever include a very small proportion of a population of a school. It could be suggested that for every child to feel valued and recognised a school has to adhere to a more far-reaching commitment and understanding as to how voices can be heard.

Key ideas: **Circle time**

How does circle time give children a voice?

Circle time is a useful vehicle for the child's voice and can be used to ensure that children feel their views are respected. It can provide a forum in which children can explore their thoughts and feelings. In addition, circle time can also aid the democratic and participative process by helping children to develop the communication skills they need to put their views across in ways that are sufficiently clear and powerful for them to be heard in other contexts like school council (Klein, 2003).

Circle time can also be very successful at dealing with problems like bad behaviour in school and friendship issues. Agendas like SEAL (Social and Emotional Aspects of Learning), which have been adopted by many schools, give very informative and practical advice as to how to go about circle time and also suggest activities that can be used to help promote productive sessions. Circle time, however, does need to be conducted with care, empathy, positivity and attention to detail. Smith notes *that unless children's feelings are handled sensitively they may have a negative impact* (2008, p.60). The same author states that the two aims of circle time are to raise self-esteem and solve emotional problems, but if children are learning a negative vocabulary then the opposite may be achieved.

Key idea: **Assessment**

How involving children in target-setting and assessment gives children a voice

Target-setting is another way children can participate in their own learning and helps give them a voice in the classroom. With the notion of assessment for learning and personalisation now increasingly common in the primary curriculum, one-on-one teacher/pupil target-setting has become a more firmly embedded phenomenon. The process by which children discuss their progression and consider a targeted course of action in order to further improve could help them to be more engaged with their learning journey than a child who is excluded from the experience. In other words, target-setting helps children to feel they have more control over their educational experience.

Klein (2003, p.86) also discusses pupils' involvement in their assessment and states that it helps children feel *empowered*. However, she adds that for this mechanism to be at all meaningful to a child the experience should be more than children coming to *tutorials*. Instead, children need to feel that they have their views listened to seriously and, as far as they are able to, engage in a joint discussion.

Key ideas: **International comparison**

How do we compare with educational systems in other parts of Europe?

At this point it is worth reviewing how schools in Europe have tackled the issues of participation and empowerment of children. The Euridem Project (Klein, 2003) investigated the theme of student participation in Denmark, Germany, Sweden and the Netherlands. The project found that the idea of student participation and the voice of children was well embedded in these countries compared to progress made in this area in UK schools. The project went on to conclude that children who experienced learning environments where their views were listened to and respected gained direct benefits for their confidence, self-esteem, behaviour and attendance, and were generally more connected with their learning. These countries delivered what is described as a *democratic* system of schooling.

In Denmark, for instance, teaching is based on a dialogic structure in which discussion is the major part of the lesson content. This is markedly different to the teaching style within classrooms in the UK in the past ten years, where emphasis on talk might be focussed on the first part of a lesson when teaching explanations take place. Interestingly, in Denmark the awarding of marks for a piece of work is less prevalent; it is the student's ability to interact in group work which is seen as a more meaningful assessment criterion (Klein, 2003). Again, this is very different from the UK education system, where there is more emphasis on levelling work and the marking of products against prescribed criteria.

In Sweden there is also a focus on democratic schooling structures. Children sit on school boards, which allow them to have a say in important issues like teacher recruitment, financial considerations and curriculum planning. Teachers even involve their children in the evaluation of their teaching (Klein, 2003). In the UK, although children are now consulted in the selection of new teaching appointments, it would not be considered routine for them to be included in the evaluation of teaching sessions; this still firmly remains in the adult arena. Children being involved in the evaluation of teaching demands the practitioner themselves to be confident, constructive, reflective and have a real commitment to the value of pupil participation.

When considering our European partners it is worth noting some other initiatives that reveal an altogether freer approach to teaching and learning and that encourage attributes that help to develop learner choice and active participation. The early advocacy of and commitment to outdoor schools and forest schools is a case in point here. These are approaches that encourage the early development of resilience, increased engagement and decision-making. The effectiveness of these schooling systems has been recognised in the UK and is now being adopted in many nursery settings and schools. While this might be considered a valuable development, it will only be

---

effective if the staff who implement these initiatives are well trained and develop a good understanding of the values and ethics that underpin these approaches. Dowling (2005) makes the valid argument that learning environments often remain places where adults dominate and put children in a position where they can only respond. Dowling (2005) also notes that children who have had their thoughts and views disregarded by adults, or have not been allowed to try things out for themselves, may learn to accept that they are not important and will therefore not feel worthy of participation.

Good practice in the early years, it could be argued, starts to produce children who have voices that are heard. For instance, play-based learning environments help to put children in control of their learning and allow them to make choices as well as provoking creative and imaginative responses (Dowling, 2005). Furthermore, the concept of *sustained shared thinking* developed through play allows children to express themselves. This term, which is emphasised in the Early Years Foundation Stage Curriculum (DCSF, 2008a), and has gained increasing prominence in the past few years, is a concept that encourages the voice of the child. This strategy develops the notion of questioning children in class and adopts the process of mutual conversations.

Dowling (2005) also notes that instances of shared talk are relatively rare in classrooms and that, although this does not call the quality of the relationships between teacher and child into question, the conversations that are had in class are often managerially based around daily routines. In contrast, practitioners who listen and respond to the interests of children are far more effective. Those practitioners who showed a genuine concern for children and used this information to gain fresh insights, reflect and move on, were more successful in making children active participants in their own learning. Dowling (2005) goes on to exemplify this by likening the learning to a game of ping-pong, where the practitioner helps a child to clarify and articulate their ideas, offers it for consideration to a wider group and allows other children to throw back their response.

Silin (2005) also writes poignantly about the role of the teacher in developing the child's voice; he combines personal and professional experiences in an exploration of the importance of silence in promoting the correct kinds of voice in the class. He notes the critical choices that practitioners make about the interplay of voice and silence, arguing that when a practitioner speaks another does not and that silence opens the space for others to announce themselves. Silin (2005) explores the value of using silence to allow children to develop an internal dialogue and notes that our eagerness to promote talk might interrupt this dialogue for children. This is a valid point and reminds us of the importance of allowing children to dwell and reflect in the educational process.

This might be illustrated with reference to the welcome development of practices that explore the potential of outdoor space for educational purposes. These areas have now been equipped with many stimulating resources, but it is as important to consider the value of spaces where children can simply sit and reflect, places where they can make sense of the rhythms and cadences of the day. As Silin (2005, p.94) puts it, *silence invites the spiritual to present itself.*

CASE STUDY

Many years ago, as a young teacher of a Year 5 class, I recall a half-term when the children undertook a sewing project. The objectives of this project had been carefully planned and I know the children produced some wonderful work, showing careful design and execution of stitch work. However, it is not the skills and objectives of this project that I remember most about this experience. When I reflect back on this, what I do recall is how much the children enjoyed this activity, which took place every week, last thing on a Friday afternoon. I wonder now what implicit messages I was giving to the children about the value I placed on this activity, having relegated it to a Friday afternoon task, postponed until the 'more important' subjects had been addressed. Nevertheless, the children looked forward to Friday afternoons as they could sit where they wanted and talk to their friends as they undertook the task.

Meanwhile, I would sit amongst the children and help them when they got into difficulties, but I was also concurrently working on my own sewing project. I would sew alongside them and vividly recall the casual talk that the children would include me in. I was a party to their incidental conversations, chatting about their likes and dislikes, hearing details about their families, their siblings, the games they were currently playing and also the songs and popstars they thought were 'cool'. I can remember how much I enjoyed these occasions where the boundaries and power inequalities between 'me', the teacher, and 'them', the learners, were temporarily blurred. It was times like these that children who found it more difficult to use their voice in class, and found it hard to contribute, might also start to speak. I can remember feeling privileged to be included in this way and these times for me became not so much about the children sewing, but about the conversations that took place.

At the same time I recall that these sessions worried me. As a new teacher I was concerned about the amount of time this activity was taking; I did not want to 'waste' curriculum time. I also worried about the unfocused nature of the talk and what other practitioners would think if they should come into my classroom at this time. I was even slightly anxious about the loss of control. While I enjoyed the conversations that were taking place, I did not see them as educational and I gave them less value than the talk that was produced in other lessons; but I do remember wishing that the voices of the children could be as fluid and unrestrained in literacy lessons as they were in sewing time. What I did not understand at that point was that a teacher should 'listen' to everything and what these sessions were doing was enabling the children to tell me the narrative of their lives and in doing so they were constructing stories. Conversations like these were allowing voices to

/continued

CASE STUDY – continued

come through loud and clear and this, in turn, would have a knock-on benefit to the development of talk and the production of the critically evaluative voice that I wanted to promote in literacy lessons. As Silin (2005) states, I was allowing my children to: *craft their own stories that would be listened to* (Silin, 2005, p.94).

A **Compare** the different and competing educational values that come through in this case study.

B **Consider** the values this case highlights that you feel to be important in working with children.

C **Explore** other ways you might be able to incorporate children's voice into your teaching.

Comment

Silin's (2005) work presents ideas similar to those explored in the case study above. He argues that the good teacher or practitioner should, at times, remain silent and listen to what the children are talking about – as doing so will, as the case study above illustrates, show how much can be learnt by listening to what children want to say and talk about as being of importance to them. In this way, when working with children it is important to consider the value placed on certain types of talk and how some types of voice may have more currency than others.

Conclusion

Schools have a much greater function than simply the transmission of knowledge; they help to educate today's children to be citizens of the future, to create young people who engage with their communities and contribute in a positive manner. For this reason educators need to embrace a philosophy that centres on participation and empowerment. After reading this chapter:

- ⊙ **analyse** how the image of children who are presented either as helpless victims or egocentric threats to society needs to be reviewed or at least examined in a critical way that seeks to understand the extent to which it reflects our own anxieties about childhood;
- ⊙ **explore** how initiatives like the UNCRC enshrine 'rights' that detail the importance of participation and of valuing the voice of the child, and how steps have been taken in schools to help develop this;
- ⊙ **consider** how many schools have started to give children a voice and responsibility through vehicles like school councils.

If schools are to be successful in making responsible future citizens, they need to place the engagement and empowerment of the child at the heart of their core ethos and philosophy.

Further Reading

Sinclair Taylor, A (2000) The UN Convention on the Rights of the Child: giving children a voice, in Lewis, A. & Lindsay, G. (eds) *Researching Children's Perspectives*. Buckingham: Open University Press. p30.

Silin, J (2005) Silence, voice and pedagogy, in Yelland, N. (ed) *Critical Issues in Early Childhood education*. Maidenhead: Open University Press. p94.

8

Ethics, values and the teacher

Glenn Stone

Chapter Focus

The critical thinking exercises in this chapter focus on:

⊙ **analysing** what form the underlying principles of the issues being discussed;
⊙ **articulating** what underpins your own approach to the issues being discussed;
⊙ **comparing** a range of approaches and outcomes;
⊙ **considering** what ideas provide the most helpful way forward to resolving conflicting situations;
⊙ **discussing** the tensions between competing ideas;
⊙ **exploring** how issues can be approached in different ways;
⊙ **imagining** different approaches to a situation.

The Key ideas discussed are: **personal ethics and values**, **schools with specific values and ethics**, **ethical commitment**, **teacher professionalism**, **professional integrity**, **utilitarianism**, **performance management**, **virtue ethics**.

This chapter is particularly relevant to Teachers' Standards: **1**, **4**, **5** and **8**.

Introduction

This book has explored ethics and values as they apply to the concepts of diversity, society, the curriculum, leadership and management, the classroom and, finally, but not least importantly, the children. Within each of these chapters and themes you have been invited to consider your own position and ethics in response to these themes. This chapter will again touch on some of the previous themes but will also highlight some other ways in which ethics and values can underpin a teacher's role. It begins by exploring how important ethics and values are when applying for a teaching post. Teachers' status as professionals is then explored and an argument is put forward that in order to maintain this status, teachers must be ethical. The ethics of teachers' accountability is also put under the spotlight in order to help the reader reflect on how this influences teachers and can force them to work through ethical dilemmas. Finally, the possibility of staying true to your ethics and values, becoming virtuous in the process, is put forward as an intrinsic part of long-term teacher success.

Key idea: **Personal ethics and values**

Sometimes different people have different ethics and values

In Chapter 1, the idea of having to reconcile tensions between personal ethics and values and those held by others was introduced. As a teacher, these tensions can appear in many guises and in many different situations on a daily basis: dealing with a behavioural problem, talking to parents at the school gate, contributing to staff or team meetings, are all examples of day-to-day microevents that consciously or unconsciously will be formed by individual ethics and values. Throughout this book we have explored many values and ethics that relate to education and the differences between what people value and believe to be the correct or incorrect way to go about things. It is part of our role in schools to be able to explain to others why we value the things we do and believe in and what we regard as the ethically correct way to do things.

As suggested in Chapter 1, ethics and values are much to do with having a considered approach to help know what is right and wrong in a given situation. However, if what you deem to be right is different to another person's view, then the strength with which you defend your decision may have a positive or negative outcome. Consider how some teachers might stringently reprimand children for not wearing the correct school uniform or having their PE kit. Strong ethics and values for upholding the uniform code and standards of presentation might help them justify their approach to this situation without considering the other factors for why the child might not be complying with the rules. What if the child ripped his school trousers and his parents were financially unable to purchase him new ones? Here the strength of a teacher's ethics and values to follow the rules could be seen as not being compassionate or aware of the child's circumstances. On the other hand, there are times when having strong ethics and values can result in positive outcomes. Consider how a school might know that a child uses racist language but turns a blind eye because they believe this racism stems from the home and there is nothing that can be done. One teacher who decides to tackle the issue because they strongly believe that the racist language is wrong could help other stakeholders in the school to change their approach to this issue.

It can be suggested that an understanding of ethics and values is particularly important when applying for a teaching post. First-time teachers are often given the advice that they should apply for schools that they would be happy working in. To achieve this, prospective teachers need to determine their teaching values and match these to a compatible school. Sometimes this is referred to as having a *teaching philosophy*, underpinned by carefully thought-through ethics and values. As ethics is concerned with knowing what is right or wrong in any given situation, the point at which a teacher is applying for a teaching post is a good time to examine the strength of their ethics, values, principles and philosophy.

Key idea: **Schools with specific values and ethics**

Some schools are founded on particular ethical values which impact on all aspects of education

Ethical absolutism, as discussed in Chapter 1, deals with absolutes: if something is right in one situation, then it is right in all situations. Arguably, teachers with strong religious faith or beliefs may adopt an absolutist approach to education and apply for jobs only in schools that share the same ethics and values. For example, a Roman Catholic with a strong faith may not consider it possible for them to teach in a Church of England school. Aside from religious-based and faith schools, some schools, such as Montessori or Steiner schools, are founded on other specific values that teachers working within them or applying for jobs at will need at least to support, if not believe and conform to. Before applying for a post in a school you might need to consider how your own values and ethics might work alongside those of the school you are applying to.

While the strength of a teacher's individual ethics and values will help them to make a decision whether or not to apply for a post in some schools that have a clearly stated approach to education, such as faith schools, other schools might have developed an 'ethos' based on the strength of an individual headteacher's ethics and values, or a core of teachers that have worked in the school for a long period of time. In these circumstances, it is again important to consider how important your own ethics and values are and the extent to which they can be compromised.

Critical thinking exercise 1

Syed is a pre-service teacher who values the creative curriculum and promotes personalised learning in his classroom. He sees a job advertised for a *dynamic school that puts children's creativity at the heart of its ethos* and arranges to meet the headteacher and view the school before putting in an application form. However, soon after entering the school for a visit, Syed believes that the school is not as it has been advertised. Displays around the school do not show signs of creativity; the desks are arranged in rows in every classroom *for behavioural reasons*; every classroom contains textbooks and the headteacher refers to these books as a great way of raising standards. After an informal discussion with the headteacher, Syed is told that he should definitely apply for the post.

Should he submit an application form?

1 **Consider** how Syed's decision could be influenced if this is the only teaching post in the area where he wants to teach.

/continued

Critical thinking exercise 1 – continued

2 **Explore** whether Syed should question his own values if the school was graded Outstanding in its most recent OfSTED report.

3 **Analyse** Syed's value for teaching creatively if the textbook approach has resulted in the school gaining high standards through Key Stage 2 National Test data.

Comment

At a basic level, the critical thinking exercise above presents a conflict between a school and an individual teacher's personal values. The extent to which one is sacrificed for the other is an example of an ethical dilemma. Arguably, the outcome of an ethical dilemma can be influenced by many factors and personal circumstances. If this is the only job available for Syed, in spite of his teaching values, the necessity to work might overpower the conviction of his ethics. Owing to this being the only job in his area, Syed might conclude: *Ethically, I disagree with the practice in this school, but I must still apply in order to secure a job.* On the other hand, Syed might decide not to apply for the job if he remains committed to his teaching values and does not want them to be sacrificed. In some ways this is similar to ethical absolutism, where an individual might believe that something is wrong and therefore it would not be ethical to be complicit in the situation. Here Syed might conclude: *Ethically, I cannot apply for this job because my values are fundamentally different to those of the school.* We might consider how happy Syed would be teaching at this school day-in, day-out if he cannot teach in the way that he believes to be appropriate. It is also interesting to consider how Syed might be influenced by the Outstanding OfSTED accolade, or the National Test data that suggest the school is doing well. Is it a teacher's ethical duty to educate the children to the best of their ability and, therefore, whatever approach leads to these results should be valued? Following this line of thinking, Syed might question his own values.

Key idea: **Ethical commitment**

Being committed to your ethics and values

Using just one example, we have seen that ethics is a complex issue and that it is possible to arrive at different outcomes, depending on which ethical stance an individual takes. It is therefore useful to consider that ethics can be used as a way of justifying, explaining and reasoning a response to any given situation. An understanding of ethics and knowing our own values can help us to explain how and why we have arrived at a decision and then justify this decision as being right or wrong in any given situation. Therefore, ethical reasoning should be viewed as a route to the answer as opposed to the answer itself. In this way it might be easier to stand by our convictions.

Continuing with the theme of applying for a job, the interview process can be an ideal opportunity for a prospective teacher to demonstrate the conviction of their ethics and values. The following critical thinking exercise illustrates this with sample questions and shows how, in responding to them, a candidate might demonstrate their values. Although the questions can also be answered with knowledge and understanding of educational theory, headteachers and interview panellists will also want to know that the candidate is right for the school. A candidate might become stronger if they can demonstrate an educational philosophy that is congruent with the school's ethos.

Critical thinking exercise 2

Possible interview questions	Values considerations
What do you think makes a successful school?	This is an ideal opportunity to show what you value about schools as a whole, your educational philosophy and how you value the children.
What are your strengths as a teacher?	What strengths do you have that will be of value to this school? How will your strengths be of value to the children and their parents?
In the long term, would you be interested in co-ordinating a curriculum subject?	Which subject do you value the most? For example, you might have a love for the arts and want this to come through in interview. Explain how your chosen subject can impact on the children's values.
Describe your perfect classroom environment.	How can you use the classroom environment to demonstrate that you value the children? Do you value your own personal organisation as a strength? What value do you place on displays in helping children to learn to celebrate their success?
How would you use the outdoor environment?	Why is the outdoors of value to children's education? If you value the outdoors in your own leisure pursuits, then show this enthusiasm here.
How will you deploy teaching assistants or other adults in your classroom?	Demonstrate the value that you place on the involvement of other adults, including parents and volunteer helpers. What contribution can they make and how will you demonstrate your appreciation of this? Use an example to illustrate how you have valued other adults in previous teaching experiences.
Why is working with parents important?	Again, demonstrate that you value the involvement of parents and the difference that they make to their child's education. Illustrate with examples if possible.

1 **Consider** your own values by working through the interview questions above.

2 Working with another person, **discuss** whether or not you would answer the questions differently and **investigate** the reasons for this.

3 **Analyse** whether you would answer the questions honestly or if you would change your answers slightly depending on the ethos and values of the school.

Comment

Although these questions might come up in an interview situation, they are also a useful framework for thinking about values at any point in your career. As time goes on, some teachers might change their values and beliefs based on their experiences. Others will not change their values and instead use them as a way of approaching different situations. The theme of how important individual ethics and values are will return throughout this chapter.

Key idea: **Teacher professionalism**

> **What is a professional and why should the job of a teacher be classified as a profession?**
>
> The term 'professional' is applied in many different situations: a business might want to project a professional image to its clients; a tradesman or woman might be considered to leave a 'professional finish' at the end of a job; sportsmen and women might be deemed 'professional' once they have started earning money from the sport as opposed to their 'amateur' colleagues. With the term being used extensively, it can be suggested that it is difficult to define exactly what 'professional', 'professionalism' and 'profession' mean. Evans (2008) concurs with this and argues that without a universally accepted definition, it is difficult to know how professionalism as a concept functions or how it can be influenced. One way of establishing whether or not someone is a professional is to consider whether professional ethics are central to their role (Carr, 2000).

Without being bound to an ethical code, the role of a teacher could arguably be quite different. If teaching is not a profession, then the ethical and moral accountability loses its significance. As it is, teaching should be classified as a profession because there is a moral, ethical code that teachers must comply with and furthermore, professional ethics should permeate everything they do. The 2012 Teachers' Standards (DfE, 2011c) make it clear that behaving ethically is a core component of the professional status of teachers:

Teachers uphold public trust in the profession and maintain high standards of ethics and behaviour, within and outside school, by:

- *treating pupils with dignity, building relationships rooted in mutual respect, and at all times observing proper boundaries appropriate to a teacher's professional position;*

- *having regard for the need to safeguard pupils' well-being, in accordance with statutory provisions;*

- *showing tolerance of and respect for the rights of others;*

- *not undermining fundamental British values, including democracy, the rule of law, individual liberty and mutual respect, and tolerance of those with different faiths and beliefs;*

- *ensuring that personal beliefs are not expressed in ways which exploit pupils' vulnerability or might lead them to break the law.*

(DfE, 2011c, p.8)

Critical thinking exercise 3

Carr states that: *There is an important ethical or moral ingredient to professional organisation, whereby someone may be judged unfit to practise professionally because, despite their possession of relevant theories and skills, they lack appropriate values, attitudes or motive* (Carr, 2000, p.25).

1 **Articulate** what Carr means by these claims.

2 **Explore** how a teacher might be *judged unfit to practise professionally.*

3 **Experiment** with how the teaching role could be different if it was a vocation or a trade.

Comment

In responding to the exercise above you might have considered different vocations or trades and attempted to draw a comparison. For example, a tradesman who advertises himself as a 'professional plumber' might be considered by many as exactly that, a professional. Others would not consider a plumber to be a professional by considering the ethics and values that underpin this job. If a professional plumber was caught guilty of wrongdoing, it is possible that they could continue to practise this career, albeit with a damaged reputation. Ethically, they might have done something wrong but they are not held accountable to a higher ethical code. In contrast, if a teacher was caught doing something that was ethically wrong, they might not be allowed to continue teaching.

In deciding how you want to be as a teacher, it can be useful to consider your own definition of what professionalism means and how it impacts on all aspects of your life. Consider before completing the following critical thinking exercise, whether or not you believe the school-based work of a teacher should impact on a teacher's personal life. In doing this, consider whether the professional ethics and values of the teaching profession pervade all aspects of your own life.

Critical thinking exercise 4

First, read this scenario:

John is an experienced teacher who works in an urban primary school with a diverse range of children. In school, he is well respected and considered to be an excellent teacher. John lives in a small rural village, outside of the town where he works. A proposal is submitted for the development of a traveller site on disused farmland in his village. John attends a meeting at the local village hall to oppose the site. Unknowingly, the local press is also at the meeting and in the next edition of the local newspaper there is a photograph of the protesters with John clearly being identifiable by the picture.

Now, consider these two statements:

- Ethical absolutism deals in absolutes; if something is right or wrong in one situation, then it is right or wrong in all situations.
- Teachers are bound by an ethical code of conduct to promote equality and diversity.

1   **Explain** the ethical dilemma that John will face when teaching. Use the term *ethical absolutism* in your explanation.

2   **Articulate** how a teacher's conduct in their personal lives can impact on the professional status of teachers as a whole.

3   **Challenge** the assumption that because teachers have met desired competencies with regards to equality and diversity they are always tolerant of different groups.

4   **Consider** whether or not a professional person should demonstrate their values at all times, including through their personal lives.

Comment

The above exercise illustrates how a teacher might not apply their ethical duties outside of the school setting and this raises questions about their professional status. This might help us to address the question of how we want to be perceived as a teacher, both individually and as a profession as a whole. Campbell (2003, p.23) argues that *[t]he ethical teacher is, by necessity, an ethical person.* The two things are not considered here to be separate and this distinction is further explored by suggesting that it is a matter of integrity:

One who lies and cheats for personal gain or who is callous towards the feelings of others is unlikely to transform into a principled person of integrity upon becoming a teacher. And, the teacher who strives to empathize with students and colleagues, who aims to be fair, careful, trustworthy, responsible, honest, and courageous in the professional role probably understands and appreciates the importance of such virtues in everyday life as well.

(Campbell, 2003, p.23)

Many would concur with Campbell's line of argument here. A teacher with integrity would apply the same moral code to their everyday life as they do in the classroom. This can be contentious for teachers that smoke, as they might find it ethically difficult to teach children the morals of not smoking, whilst not applying this to their own situation. Many people will be familiar with a 'do as I say, not as I do' argument, and this is not necessarily going to contribute to personal integrity. Here we are moving away from dealing in absolutes and suggesting that it is possible to separate an individual's role as a teacher and their everyday life, but in doing so, the individual has to work through their ethics in order to justify their decisions. Returning to John, his appearance in the newspaper suggests that he is against a traveller site and this is in conflict with his job as a teacher to promote equality and diversity. Therefore, it is difficult to conclude that he could transform into an ethical teacher when entering school. Consider how John would be perceived by any children of traveller heritage in his school if they thought that he was campaigning against a traveller site. Even if there were no children of traveller heritage, John has a professional duty to set a good example and be a positive role model for the children. In this professional capacity, what example would be set to the children if they considered him to be intolerant of others?

Key idea: **Professional integrity**

What does it mean for a teacher to have professional integrity?

In order to have professional integrity, a teacher should act ethically. Others will perceive an individual teacher as having integrity if this virtue has been earned. In order to gain or maintain professional integrity, an individual must be seen to be making the right decisions and behaving ethically. There is no single thing that a teacher can do to have integrity; integrity derives from everything a teacher does. This includes treating children fairly, demonstrating values for social justice, raising children's self-esteem, and so on. Although a teacher will be perceived as having integrity from what they do, their actions should be underpinned by strong values and ethics for what is right or wrong. In this way, it would be difficult to argue that a teacher has professional integrity if there is disparity between their personal and professional ethics.

Teachers, as professionals, are held accountable in a variety of ways. As explored in previous chapters, much of this accountability is concerned with the standards agenda. Here we will look at how the standards agenda affects teachers through their performance management objectives and the ethics of such an approach.

Key idea: **Utilitarianism**

What is utilitarianism?

Utilitarianism is a branch of consequentialist ethics, and as such, deals with the consequences of actions. Jeremy Bentham, the originator of this theory, argued that human decisions are founded on maximising pleasure and reducing pain. This is known as the *principle of utility*. The theory has been developed and adopted by governments as an ideology suggesting that society should generate overall benefits with limited negative consequences. Therefore, actions should contribute to the greater good. Many utilitarians believe that the wellbeing and happiness of mankind should be the main outcome of utilitarianism. However, as Furrow (2005) argues, happiness is difficult to define and what is classified as the greater good can also be subjective. This ethical approach could seem appealing to teachers as they strive to maximise the happiness and wellbeing of their class. To illustrate this, consider how a teacher might work hard and spend a lot of their personal time at a weekend planning and resourcing an exciting series of lessons for the following week. The loss of a teacher's personal time could result in many children having a greater experience when the lessons are taught. Therefore, the principle of utility has been applied successfully because the positive benefits for the class outweigh the negative consequences for the teacher.

Happiness and wellbeing can be regarded as long term benefits that develop from having a good education, as well as the short-term happiness that a child might experience as a member of the school community. In this way, the government's standards agenda could be viewed as providing long term wellbeing. The argument could be that if the majority of primary school children are educated to a high standard then society as a whole will benefit from having a more academic workforce. Therefore schools and teachers are tasked to raise standards and are set targets for meeting these. As a result, teachers are held accountable to these standards through mechanisms such as performance management.

Key idea: **Performance management**

What is performance management?

Performance management is a system where teachers are given individual targets and objectives that are linked to the outcomes of their children's learning. Examples of a performance management target could be for a teacher to ensure that 75 per cent of their class make half a level progress in maths, or that all children, excluding those with special educational needs, make the expected progress in writing. Within the principle of utility, the setting of targets that benefit the majority of children seems to be a positive outcome. If a Year 6 teacher is told that they must ensure that 80 per cent of their children achieve a Level 4 in writing, the teacher could target those most likely to make this progress and 'pitch' their lessons accordingly. Here the focus on raising the standards of the majority is acceptable both in terms of the performance management objective and utilitarianism.

Like all branches of ethics, utilitarianism is not without its limitations. The problem of utilitarian ethics is that the negative consequences of actions, however severe, do not matter as long as the positive outcomes outweigh the negative. Furrow (2005, p. 46) illustrates the problem of utilitarianism by stating that *if society as a whole benefits enough from slavery, it would outweigh the negative consequences on the slaves.* Our common sense morality and understanding of social justice would lead us to believe that, in this instance, utilitarianism is not the most ethical approach. Returning then to performance management and the standards agenda, if a teacher is tasked with ensuring that the majority of children make expected progress, there is a danger that the minority will be excluded. These exclusive practices that contradict a teacher's ethical duty to value all children have been found to occur in primary schools, particularly in Year 6 in the lead-up to National Tests (Hall *et al.*, 2004). This time in a school year can show the direct consequence of teachers' (and by association, schools') performance management objectives as the teachers will be striving to achieve high standards for the majority of children. This study finds that a school's organisation, their approach towards the tests and the general rhetoric at this time of year results in exclusive education:

 Practice tends, unsurprisingly, towards that which is perceived to have the greatest consequences for the survival and status of the school itself, namely, competitive league table performance which in turn seems to push towards ability grouping, testing and competition, thus making for a climate of exclusive practices.

(Hall *et al.*, 2004, p.815)

Within this study, the school is concerned with the wellbeing of the school as a whole, namely its *survival and status* (p.815). The principle of utility, applied here, would suggest that the net benefit gained from the long-term survival of the school is worthy of any short-term negative consequences to some of the children. Therefore, the *climate of exclusive practices* (p.815) might be viewed as being a necessary negative consequence in order to achieve the greater good. Moreover, the outcome of these measures could lead to higher standards, resulting in long-term educational benefits for the children. However, the ethical dilemma that utilitarianism presents here is whether or not it is right for teachers to endorse the repression of a specific group (such as those not able to achieve the school's standards) for the greater good of the school? Should the teacher be equitable towards all children in the class, even if this has a detrimental effect on the wider school?

Critical thinking exercise 5

Kate is teaching in Year 6 and is a couple of months away from the National Tests. She has been told by the headteacher that the school's priority is boys' writing and that this group will make the difference to the school's Key Stage 2 data. Kate has been given a performance management objective to raise the standards of boys and has been told that if she achieves this target, she will be eligible for a threshold payment (a higher salary for being considered as a teacher with additional experience and competency).

Kate has noticed that after a lot of emphasis on the boys, there is a small group of girls that are falling behind and she is worried that they will not reach their full potential in the forthcoming tests. She speaks to the head about her concern but is told that all resources (T.A. time, booster groups, etc.) must be directed to the boys as they are the main priority.

1 **Articulate** Kate's ethical dilemma.

2 **Explore** what you would do in Kate's position.

3 **Imagine** a range of ways Kate could deal with this situation.

Comment

So, as teachers strive to achieve their performance management objective or raise standards, the challenge is to ensure that all children still succeed. In Chapter 1 we discussed the notion of duty as an ethical approach to education; in further exploring Kant's notion of duty, Furrow (2005, p.51) explains that Kant's theory and ethics *will forbid the sacrifice of individuals for the common good*. Therefore, to focus on a specific group, or the majority but in doing so, excluding another, is not being fair to all. The dichotomy between utilitarianism (working towards the greater good of the school) and Kantian ethics (all people are of value) could in some cases present teachers with an ethical dilemma when they are under pressure to meet performance management objectives and targets. Kant's ethics of duty also suggests that people should do what is morally good. As

---

teachers, our understanding of inclusion fits within these ethics. Teachers should ensure that all barriers to learning are removed so that all children are included. This is part of a teacher's duty within the education profession. However, if a teacher's performance management objective does not target the majority of the class, there is a chance that the teacher could direct resources and objectives towards this group at the expense of another group. Focusing on a specific group of children can therefore be perceived as undermining a teacher's duty to educate all of the children in the class.

Another form of accountability comes through OfSTED inspections. The final part of this book begins by looking at what happens when OfSTED and teachers have contrasting values and explores the possibility for alternative approaches to being judged as a teacher. Early OfSTED inspections were associated with teacher anxiety and resulted in teacher stress for some individuals (Carlyle and Woods, 2002). The reason for this was that the underpinning values of OfSTED were at odds with that of the teaching profession. Through examining the impact of contrasting values between two different bodies, as Carlyle and Woods have done, it is clear to see why values in education are so significant.

Critical thinking exercise 6

Look at the following table adapted from Carlyle and Woods (2002):

OfSTED values	Teacher values
Knowledge	
Prescribed/controlled National Curriculum	Negotiated NC/flexible, autonomous practices
Emphasis on products (National Tests)	Emphasis on process
Subject-based curriculum	Child-centred, holistic, integrative
Systemisation, standardisation, uniformity	Differences, diversity
Pedagogy	
Transmissional	Creative
Behaviourist	Constructivist learning theory
Formal contexts	Informal contexts
Examination	Support
Instant performance	Learning takes time
Assessment	
Formal	Informal
Quantitative	Qualitative
Standardisation	Localised
Periodic tests	Continuous
Hierarchical examination	Collective engagement, self-assessment
Simplicity	Complexity

/continued

Critical thinking exercise 6 – continued

OfSTED values	Teacher values
Culture	
Competition	Collegiality
Blame	Support
Managerialism	Professionalism
Control	Self-regulation
Consumer	Producer

(After Carlyle and Woods, 2002, pp.138–9)

1 **Compare** the early OfSTED values with the teacher values and explore your own values as a result.

2 **Consider** which of the early OfSTED values are still prominent today.

3 **Experiment** with ways that a teacher could maintain their values whilst appeasing OfSTED.

Comment

In the critical thinking exercise above, the values are those of earlier OfSTED inspectors and inspections. When trying to form a teacher identity, some teachers might consider whether their identity is one that external bodies would impose upon them or if it is an identity formed elsewhere. Although it can be argued that OfSTED's values have evolved over the years, the exercise has been placed here to remind us how teachers' values can be vulnerable to external demands. This argument is developed by Leaton Gray (2006, p.166), who suggests that teachers have to be *infinitely retainable, responding immediately to direction from government,* and this can be evidenced by the numerous revisions to the OfSTED framework that is used to inspect schools. Changes to the OfSTED framework have resulted in the status of schools and, subsequently, the perceptions of teachers, changing in response. This can have detrimental effects, as seen in 2010 when the OfSTED framework being used at that time led to an increase in schools being judged as *inadequate* (BBC, 2010b). So, hypothetically, it is possible for a teacher to be classified as 'satisfactory' under one regime and 'inadequate' under another. The usefulness of an OfSTED criterion to judge teaching could therefore be viewed as an unreliable mechanism as the goalposts for the different grades of teacher change periodically.

Moreover, the OfSTED criteria might give a snapshot of teaching skills and performance at any given time but they do not show anything about the character, attitudes or motives of the teacher. Perhaps then, rather than simply conforming to the latest incarnation of a teacher's role in accordance with external bodies, teachers should be the teacher that they want to be, based on their ethics and values. One way of doing this is by knowing and staying true to your virtues.

Key idea: **Virtue**

What do virtue ethics mean?

As touched on in Chapter 1, virtue ethics derive from the work of Greek philosophers and aristocrats such as Aristotle. Being virtuous involves becoming a good person or having a good character as a result of holding positive virtues. These virtues have to include character traits that others would consider to be of value. Being virtuous also means that an individual does the right thing for the right reason, or motive. Therefore, a teacher might help a child to read because they care about the child and want them to succeed in life. This is a virtuous act built on the virtues of kindness and compassion. However, if a teacher helps a child to read only because this is their job and they will be rewarded financially, then the motivation for the act is not virtuous.

An act can only be virtuous if it is consistently in line with the virtues that a person possesses. To illustrate this, consider how a teacher might always use sanctions to discipline a class but for one child, their favourite, they use rewards as a motivating strategy. The kindness demonstrated to their favourite child is not replicated in their behaviour with the other children and, therefore, the teacher is not virtuous. For this reason, Furrow (2005) suggests that in virtue ethics the focus should shift away from an individual's actions and focus instead on their virtues and character traits. With this in mind, it is useful to consider how someone could become a virtuous teacher.

The desire to become virtuous can be aligned with the desire to become a better person. Within the classroom, a teacher might aspire to be a better practitioner, but how can this be achieved? One possibility is to reflect on the virtues you currently possess and consider the virtues of others, including ideal teachers. You might then begin to emulate aspects of their character and start to embody their virtuous qualities. Finally, others might recognise and identify you as being a virtuous individual.

Critical thinking exercise 7

1   **Imagine** an ideal teacher. This could be based on a teacher you have known or the teacher that you would like to be.

2   **Investigate** what virtues this teacher has and how their actions can consistently demonstrate these character traits.

3. If you aspire to be this teacher, **compare** your own virtues and explore ways that you could develop them further.

Comment

This final critical thinking exercise should help you arrive at the end of your journey through this book. Looking back over all of the chapters, consider how your own values with regard to social justice, diversity, the curriculum, the children and your role in society's wider conceptualisation of teaching impact on how you want to be as a teacher. Which virtues do you hold that others will value in you?

The importance of values and virtues can be seen through examining a teacher who is towards the end of his or her career. The following case study is based on a real teacher and illustrates how these values and virtues can be at the heart of what any teacher does.

CASE STUDY

For more than 30 years, Maggie has worked in the same school, but in this time she has worked for numerous head and deputy headteachers. Having been a teacher all her life, Maggie has lived and worked through the policies, initiatives and guidance from both Conservative and Labour governments. Consequently, she has also experienced different manifestations of OfSTED frameworks and accountability procedures. However, throughout the ever-changing political and local context of education, Maggie has kept true to her own values and virtues.

Maggie believes that her values are not necessarily different from those of any other teacher. First and foremost, she believes that the children in her care should be taught to the best of her ability and that each individual child should reach their full potential. Her dedication to the children in her class is a virtue that is demonstrated every day as she differentiates the learning and strives for high standards from all of her class. These high standards are not as a result of being given a performance management objective, a relatively recent development in her career; Maggie's high standards stem from a deep-rooted belief that the concepts of education and learning are of value in themselves.

Another long-held virtue that Maggie possesses is her compassion and kindness to the children. She believes that children should be happy at school. By getting to know the children, their interests and listening to them, Maggie raises their self-esteem because they know that they are important to her. Again, this is part of who Maggie is as a person, not just an act arising from government guidance, such as 'Every Child Matters'. To Maggie, every child has always mattered and has done long before teachers were directed in this way.

The school in which Maggie works has changed a lot over the years that she has worked there. She has experienced an ethos of collegiality when teachers have worked together and she has witnessed an ethos of competitiveness when

/continued

CASE STUDY – continued

teachers have been placed under external and internal pressures. Maggie has also been asked to deliver policies and initiatives that she has disagreed with. For example, when the National Strategies were brought in during the early Labour government years, Maggie had already proven herself as having a good track record for teaching Maths and English successfully and for raising standards. Suddenly, she was expected to ensure that every lesson objective had to emerge from the Literacy and Numeracy Strategy, even though she believed that some year group expectations were not appropriate for the children that she taught. Furthermore, when senior leaders observed Maggie they expected to see the lesson divided into the appropriate parts of the literacy and numeracy hours. Sometimes, Maggie felt that this approach was not ideal and she longed for more freedom and creativity and to be able to teach in the way that she felt was most appropriate. Maggie has found it difficult in times when her values have been compromised but when this has happened, she has tried to bring out other values to compensate. This meant that although she felt restrained by the strategies' teaching objectives, she would try to deliver them in an exciting way for the children. The virtues of obedience and loyalty to the school and headteacher balanced with the virtues of discernment and empathy with the children became a formula for Maggie's thinking at this time.

Finally, Maggie has devoted her life to the teaching profession. Devotion is a virtue that is applicable in Maggie's case because she has remained true to her vision of what makes a good teacher throughout her career. She has not allowed governmental or local changes to her school context to prevent her from doing the job that she has been committed to.

All of these virtues have resulted in Maggie not only being able to teach throughout some challenging times, but have also gained her a virtuous reputation amongst the local community and parents. She is considered to be a trustworthy, diligent and kind teacher with professional integrity.

Comment

Maggie's case study might resonate with other experienced teachers working in primary schools. Maggie has lived through a professional journey and used her virtues, ethics and values to work through the decisions that she has made. Of course, Maggie would willingly identify aspects of her practice that have not been virtuous and it is important to recognise that no one is without flaws. However, we can all strive to build on the positive virtues that we possess. In doing so, the children in our care might recognise us as being someone they look up to and admire. Consequently, the teacher acts as a role model and, as such, the virtues and values they possess can help shape children's own moral and philosophical development.

Conclusion

The aim of this chapter, and indeed the whole book, has been to invite you to:

- ⊙ **analyse** a range of ideas relating to the values and ethics inherent in education;
- ⊙ **explore** your own stance with regard to the ideas discussed; and
- ⊙ **consider** what you value as a teacher and how that will impact on the ethics that underpin how you go about your teaching.

In order to develop a philosophy, it has been argued that you need to identify your values and, within this chapter, what values and virtues you also possess. Each day a teacher has to make decisions and these will be influenced by values. Many individuals will know their values already but might not consider the extent to which they underpin everything they do, inside and outside the classroom, while embodying the professional status of a teacher. The values that we have developed and continue to develop can be demonstrated through our actions. If these actions not only present themselves in what we do as teachers but also stem from who we are as individuals, then we are on the path to becoming an ethical teacher.

Further Reading

Campbell, E (2003) *Ethical teacher.* Maidenhead: Open University Press.
Carr, D (2000) *Professionalism and ethics in teaching.* London: Routledge.
Furrow, D (2005) *Ethics: Key concepts in philosophy.* London: Continuum.

References

Acker, S and Armenti, C (2004) Sleepless in academia. *Gender and Education,* 16(1).

Acker, S and Feuerverger, G (1996) Doing good and feeling bad: the work of women university teachers. *Cambridge Journal of Education,* 26(3): 401–422.

Adams, JM and Carfagna, A (2006) *Coming of age in a globalized world: The next generation.* Bloomfield, CT, USA: Kumarian Press.

Albertson FM and Worthington, K (eds) (2009) *What is right for children?* Abingdon: Ashgate.

Alexander, R (2008) *The Primary Review. Emerging perspectives on childhood.* Online. **www.primaryreview.org.uk/Downloads/Childhood_Well-being_ and_Primary_Education_Robin_Alexander_lecture_170308.pdf** (Accessed Aug 2011)

Alexander, R (2009) *Introducing the Cambridge Review.* Online. **www. primaryreview.org.uk/downloads/CPR_revised_booklet.pdf** (Accessed October 2011).

Alexander, R (ed) (2010) *Children, their world, their education.* London: Routledge.

Amnesty International (2011) Online. **www.action.amnesty.org.uk** (accessed 7 November 2011).

Ashley, M and Nicholson, M (2008) What makes a pedagogy fit for Key Stage 2?, in Harnett, P (ed) *Understanding primary education.* London: Routledge, Taylor and Francis. pp54–71.

Audi, R (2007) *Moral value and human diversity.* New York: Oxford University Press.

Bailey, A and Barnes, S (2008) Children's futures, our futures. Educating citizens for the twenty-first century, in Harnett, P (ed) *Understanding primary education.* London: Routledge, Taylor and Francis.

Ball, SJ (2003) The teacher's soul and the terrors of performativity. *Journal of Education Policy,* 18(2): 215–28.

Ball, SJ (1994) *Education reform:* A critical and post-structural approach. Buckingham: Open University Press.

Ball, SJ (2007) Education plc: Understanding private sector participation in public sector education. Abingdon: Routledge.

BBC (2010a) 'Homosexuals not welcome' say couple who want to foster. Online. **http://news.bbc.co.uk/local/lancashire/hi/people_and_places/ newsid_8900000/8900453.stm** (accessed 9 April 2011).

BBC (2010b) More schools likely to fail under new inspections. Online. **http:// news.bbc.co.uk/1/hi/education/8558036.stm** (accessed 6 October 2011).

BBC (2011) Children 'not exercising enough'. Online. **http://news.bbc.co.uk/1/hi/ health/8015875.stm** (accessed 20 February 2012).

Beales, D (2005) *Enlightenment and reform in eighteenth-century Europe.* London: I.B. Tauris.

Benn, P (1998) *Ethics.* London: UCL Press.

Bensimon, EM, Gade, ML and Kauffman, JF (1989) *Making sense of administrative leadership: The 'L' word in higher education.* Washington, DC: ASHE/ERIC Higher Education Report No.1.

Berliner, W (2011) Guardian survey finds teachers want to be treated as professionals. Online. **www.guardian.co.uk/education/2011/oct/03/ teacher-survey-professionals-bullying-parents** (accessed 15 December 2011).

Blackmore, J (1999) *Troubling Women. Feminism, leadership and educational change.* Buckingham: Open University Press.

Blackmore, J and Sachs, J (2007) *Performing and reforming leaders: Gender, educational restructuring and organizational change.* Albany, NY: State University of New York Press.

Bourdieu, P and Passeron, JC (1977) *Reproduction in education, society and culture.* London: Sage.

Brooker, L (2008) *Supporting transitions in the early years.* Maidenhead: Open University Press.

Brooks, JG and Brooks, MG (1999) *In search of understanding: The case for constructivist classrooms* (with a new introduction by the authors). Alexandria, VA: Association for Supervision and Curriculum Development.

Bryman, A (1992) *Charisma and leadership in organisations,* London: Sage.

Campbell, E (2003) *Ethical teacher.* Maidenhead: McGraw–Hill Education.

Campbell, E (2003) *Ethical teacher.* Maidenhead: Open University Press.

Carlyle, D and Woods, P (2002) *Emotions of teacher stress.* Stoke-on-Trent: Trentham Books.

Carr, D (2000) *Professionalism and Ethics in Teaching.* London: Routledge.

CfSA (Council for Subject Associations) (2011) *Putting subjects at the core of the curriculum.* Online. **www.subjectassociation.org.uk/files/webdocs/Cfsa%20 subjects%20thinkpiece%20Mar%202011.pdf** (accessed October 2011).

Children Act 2004. c. 31. London: HMSO.

Church of England (2011) Education: Frequently asked question about church schools. Online. **www.churchofengland.org/education/ faqs.aspx#fullcurriculum** (accessed 3 November 2011).

Clarke, J and Newman, J (1997) *The managerial state.* London: Sage.

Cole, G (2004) *Management: theory and practice.* London: Thomson Learning.

Collard, J (2005) Does Size Matter?, in Collard, J and Reynolds, C (eds) *Leadership and culture in education: Male and female perspectives.* Maidenhead: Open University Press.

Collard, J and Reynolds, C (eds) (2005) *Leadership and culture in education: Male and female perspectives.* Maidenhead: Open University Press.

Court, MR (2005) Negotiating and reconstructing gendered leadership in Collard, J and Reynolds, C (eds) *Leadership and culture in education: Male and Female Perspectives.* Maidenhead: Open University Press.

Covey, S (1992) *Principle-centred leadership.* London: Simon & Schuster UK.

Cox, S, Schweisfurth, M, Dyer, C., and Robinson-Pant, A (eds) (2010) *Children as decision makers in education: Sharing experiences across cultures.* London: Continuum.

Craft, A (2000) *Creativity across the primary curriculum: Framing and developing practice.* London: RoutledgeFalmer.

Cross, G (2004) *Cute and the cool: Wondrous innocence and modern American children's culture.* Cary, NC: Oxford University Press.

Crotty, M (2003) *The foundations of social research.* London: Sage.

Curtis, W and Pettigrew, A (2009) *Learning in contemporary culture.* Exeter: Learning Matters.

Davies, B (2003) Death to critique and dissent? The policies and practices of new managerialism and of 'evidence-based practice.' *Gender and Education,* 15(1):91–103.

DCSF (Department for Children, Schools and Families) (2007) *Primary framework for literacy and mathematics.* Online. **http://webarchive.nationalarchives. gov.uk/20100202100434/nationalstrategies.standards.dcsf.gov.uk/ node/84445** (accessed November 2011).

DCSF (Department for Children, Schools and Families) (2008a) *Practice guidance for the early years Foundation Stage: Setting the standards for learning, development and care for children from birth to five.* London: DCSF.

DCSF (Department for Children, Schools and Families) (2008b) *The Early Years Foundation Stage Cards.* Online. **www.education.gov.uk/publications/standard/ publicationDetail/Page1/DCSF-00261-2008** (accessed September 2011).

Dewey, J (1897) *My pedagogic creed.* Online. **http://dewey.pragmatism.org/creed. htm** (accessed August 2011).

Dewey, J. (1916[1966]). *Democracy and education: An introduction to the philosophy of education.* New York: Free Press [Macmillan].

DfE (Department for Education) (2010) *The importance of teaching The Schools White Paper.* London: TSO. Online. **www.education.gov.uk/schools/ teachingandlearning/schoolswhitepaper/b0068570/ the-importance-of-teaching/** (accessed October 2011).

DfE (Department for Education) (2011a) *Behaviour and discipline in schools. A guide for head teachers and schools staff.* London: DfE.

DfE (Department for Education) (2011b) *Ensuring good behaviour in schools: A summary for head teachers, governing bodies, teachers, parents and pupils.* London: DfE.

DfE (Department for Education) (2011c) *Teachers' Standards.* Effective from 1 September 2012 London: DfE. Online. **http://media.education.gov.uk/assets/ files/pdf/t/teachers%20standards.pdf** (accessed 29 October 2011).

DfE (Department for Education) (2011c) *Teachers' Standards.* Effective from 1 September 2012. Online. **http://media.education.gov.uk/assets/files/pdf/t/ teachers%20standards.pdf** (accessed 6 October 2011).

DfE (Department for Education) (2012) Website Welcome page. Online. **www.education.gov.uk** (accessed 9 October 2011).

DfEE (Department of Education and Employment) (1998) *The National Literacy Strategy.* London: DfEE.

DfEE (Department of Education and Employment) (1999) *The National Numeracy Stategy.* London: DfEE.

DFEE (Department of Education and Employment) and QCA (Qualifications and Curriculum Authority) (1999) *The National Curriculum.* London: DfEE/QCA.

DfES (Department of Education and Skills) (2004) *Every Child Matters.* London: TSO.

Dowling. M (2005) *Young children's personal, social and emotional development.* London: Sage.

Dreier, J (ed) (2006) *Contemporary debates in moral theory.* Oxford: Blackwell.

Drummond, A, Duckett, R, Holland, W, Gura, P, Lockett, A, Maxwell S, Penn, H, Pound, L, Santer, J, Sellick, D and Whalley, M (1997) *Reflections on early education and care inspired by visits to Reggio Emilia, Italy.* London: Early Education.

DSCF (Department for Children, Schools and Families) (2009) *Independent Review of the Primary Curriculum: Final report.* Online. **www.education.gov. uk/publications/eOrderingDownload/Primary_curriculum_Report.pdf** (accessed October 2011).

Dubrin, A (1995) *Leadership: Research findings, practice and skills.* Boston, MA: Houghton Mifflin.

Equality Act 2010. c. 15. London: HMSO.

Equality and Human Rights Commission (2011) Introduction to the equality duty. Online. **www.equalityhumanrights.com/advice-and-guidance/public-sector-equality-duty/introduction-to-the-equality-duty/** (accessed February 2012).

Evans, L. (2008). Professionalism, professionality and the development of education professionals. *British Journal of Educational Studies,* 56(1): 20–38.

Farrell, M (1999) *Key issues for primary schools.* London: Routledge.

Fieldwork Education (no date) *The International Primary Curriculum.* Online. **http://www.internationalprimarycurriculum.com/view_page. php?page=privacy** (accessed 2011).

Fisch, K and Mcleod, S (2007) *Did you know shift happens. Globalisation and the information age.* Online. **www.youtube.com/watch?v=ljbI-363A2Q** (accessed October 2011).

Forester, G. (2003) Performance and professionalism: an exploration of primary school teachers' perspectives of the 'new managerialism'. Unpublished Ph.D thesis, Keele University.

Forrester, G. (2005) All in a day's work: primary teachers 'performing' and 'caring'. *Gender and Education* 17(3): 271–87.

Fowler, RB and Hertzke, AD (2009) *Religion and politics in America: Faith, culture, and strategic choices,* 4th edn. Boulder, CO: Westview Press.

Fullan, M (2001) *Leading in a culture of change.* San Francisco: Jossey-Bass.

Furrow, D (2005) *Ethics: Key concepts in philosophy.* London: Continuum.

Gaine, C (2005) *We're all white thanks.* Stoke-on-Trent: Trentham Books.

Gardner, H (1993) *Frames of mind,* 2nd edn. London: Fontana Press.

Garner, S (2007) *Whiteness.* Abingdon: Routledge.

Gewirtz, S. (1997) The education market, labour relations in schools and teacher unionism in the UK, in Glatter, R, Woods, PA and Bagley, C (eds) *Choice and diversity in schooling: Perspectives and prospects.* London: Routledge.

Gewirtz, S. (2002) *The managerial school: Post-welfarism and social justice in education.* London: Routledge.

Grainger, T and Barnes, J (2006) Creativity in the primary curriculum, in Arthur J, Grainger, T and Wray D (eds) *Learning to teach in the primary school.* London: Routledge. pp.209–25.

Gray, M and Webb, SA (2010) *Ethics and value perspectives in social work.* Basingstoke: Palgrave Macmillan.

Hall, K, Collins, J, Benjamin, S, Nind, M and Sheehy, K (2004) SATurated models of pupildom: assessment and inclusion/exclusion. *British Educational Research Journal.* 30(6): 801–17

Hallam, S and Rogers, L (2008) *Improving behaviour and attendance at school.* Buckingham: Open University Press.

Halocha, J (2002) *Geographical Enquiry,* in Johnston, J, Chater, M, and Bell, D (eds) *Teaching the primary curriculum.* Buckingham: Open University Press. pp.161–74.

Harnett, A and Naish, M (1990) The sleep of reason breeds monsters: the birth of a statutory curriculum in England and Wales. *Journal of Curriculum Studies,* 22(1): 1–16.

Harris, A (2008) *Distributed school leadership.* London: Routledge.

Harris, A and Lambert, L (2003) *Building leadership capacity for school improvement.* Maidenhead: Open University Press.

Hinman, LM (2003) *Ethics: A pluralistic approach to moral theory.* Belmont, CA: Wadsworth–Thompson

Husbands, C (1982) *'Race' in Britain – Continuity and change.* London: Hutchinson.

Jordan, A, Carlile, O and Stack, A (2008) *Approaches to learning: A guide for teachers.* Maidenhead: Open University Press.

Kehily, M (2008) *Introduction to childhood studies.* Maidenhead: Open University Press.

Kershaw, A (2010) *Tough new targets for underperforming schools.* Online. **www.independent.co.uk/news/education/education-news/tough-new-targets-for-underperforming-schools-2142369.html** (accessed 15 December 2011).

Klein, R (2003) *We want our say. Children as active participants in their education.* Stoke-on-Trent: Trentham Books.

Knowles, G (2009) *Ensuring every child matters.* London: Sage.

Kotter, J (1990) *A force for change: How leadership differs from management.* New York: Free Press.

Lal, BM (2006) *Educational philosophy*. Delhi: Global Media.

Lawton, D (1980) *The politics of the school curriculum*. London: Routledge.

Leaton Gray, S (2006) *Teachers under siege*. Stoke-on-Trent: Trentham Books.

Loveys, K and Roberts, H (2011) Is this what you want YOUR five-year-old learning about sex? Explicit materials cleared for schools. Online. **www.dailymail. co.uk/news/article-1364360/Sex-education-Do-want-5-year-old-child-given-explicit-lessons.html#ixzz1cYsdBiel** (accessed 3 November 2011).

Mac an Ghaill, M (1994) *The making of men: Masculinities, sexualities and schooling*. Buckingham: Open University Press.

Mahony, P and Hextall, I (2000b) *Reconstructing teaching: Standards, performance and accountability*. London: Routledge.

Martino, W (2001) 'Dickheads, wuses and faggots': Addressing issues of masculinity and homophobia in the critical literacy classroom, in Comber, B and Simpson, A (eds) *Negotiating critical literacies in classrooms*. Mahwah, NJ: Lawrence Erlbaum. pp.171–87.

Middlehurst, R (1997) Leadership, women and higher education, in Eggins, H (ed) *Women as leaders and managers in higher education*. Buckingham: Society for Research into Higher Education and Open University Press.

Mirza, H. (2009) *Race, gender and educational desire*. Abingdon: Routledge.

Morgan, R (2007a) *About education: A children's views report*. Newcastle upon Tyne: Commission for Social Care Inspection/Office of the Children's Rights Director.

Morgan, R (2007b) *The new basics: changing curriculum for the 21st century skills*. Online. **http://archive.futurelab.org.uk/resources/publications-reports-articles/vision-magazine/VISION-Article254** (accessed October 2011).

Moyles, J (2005) (ed) *Excellence of play*, 2nd edn. Maidenhead: McGraw-Hill Education.

NACCCE (National Advisory Committee on Creative and Cultural Education) (1999) All our futures: Creativity, culture and education. Report to the Secretary of State for Education and Employment and the Secretary for Culture, Media and Sport. London: NACCCE.

NICCY (Northern Ireland Commissioner for Children and Young People) (2009) *Children's Rights*. Online. **http://www.niccy.org/ChildrensRights** (accessed July 2011).

Noddings, N (1992) *The challenge to care in schools: An alternative approach to education*. New York: Teachers' College Press.

NSPCC (2009) *Feel safe at home. What to do if violence is happening around you*. London: NSPCC.

Office of the Children's Rights Director (2011) *Children on family justice*. Online. **www.rights4me.org/home/library/report-children-on-family-justice.aspx** (accessed 20 October 2011).

Office of the United Nations High Commissioner for Human Rights (2009) *Conventions on the Rights of the Child*. Online. **www2.ohchr.org/english/law/crc.htm** (accessed July 2011).

OfSTED (2002a) Creative Partnerships: Initiative and impact. The impact of sustained partnerships between schools and creative practitioners as a result of Creative Partnerships initiatives. London: OfSTED.

OfSTED (2002b) *The curriculum in successful primary schools.* London: OfSTED .

OfSTED (2007) *Early years: Getting on well: enjoying, achieving and contributing.* London: OfSTED.

OfSTED (2009a) *Care and prejudice: A report of children's experience by the Children's Rights Director for England.* Manchester: OfSTED.

OfSTED (2009b) *Twenty outstanding primary schools. Excelling against the odds.* Manchester: OfSTED.

OfSTED (2009c) *Supporting young carers. Identifying, assessing and meeting the needs of young carers and their families.* London: OfSTED.

OfSTED (2010a) *Children missing from education: The actions taken to prevent children from missing education or becoming 'lost to the system'.* Manchester: OfSTED.

OfSTED (2010b) *Learning: creative approaches that raise standards.* Online. **www.ofsted.gov.uk/node/2405** (accessed February 2012).

OfSTED (2012) *The framework for school inspection. Guidance and grade descriptors for inspecting schools in England under section 5 of the Education Act 2005, from January 2012.* Manchester: OfSTED.

Ozga, J (1993) (ed) *Women in educational management.* Buckingham: Open University Press.

Palmer, S (2006) *Toxic childhood. How the modern world is damaging our children and what we can do about it.* London: Orion Books.

Parekh, B (2000) *The future of multi-ethnic Britain.* The Parekh Report. London: The Runnymede Trust.

Peters, RS (1970) *Ethics and education.* Oxford: George Allen and Unwin.

Power, M (1994) *The audit explosion.* London: Demos.

Prensky, M (2001) Digital natives. Digital immigrants. *On the Horizon,* 9(5). Available at **www.marcprensky.com** (accessed 6 February 2012).

Prichard, C (1996) Managing universities: is it men's work?, in Collinson, DL and Hearn, J (eds) *Men as managers, men as men. Critical perspectives on men, masculinities and managements.* London: Sage.

Pring, R (2005) *Philosophy of education: Aims, theory, common sense and research.* London: Continuum.

Priola, V (2007) Being female doing gender: narratives of women in education management. *Gender and Education,* 19(1).

Puri, U (2006) *Education: theory and practice.* Delhi: Global Media.

Purshouse, L (2010) *Plato's Republic.* London: Continuum International Publishing.

QCA (Qualifications and Curriculum Authority) (1998) *Schemes of work for Key Stages 1 and 2.* London: QCA.

Reay, D and Ball, S (2000) Essentials of female management: Women's ways of working in the education market place? *Educational Management,* 28(2): 145–159. London: Sage, 5.

Renold, E (2001) Learning the 'hard' way: Boys, hegemonic masculinity and learner identities in the primary school. *British Journal of Sociology of Education*, 22(3): 369–388.

Roche, J, Tucker, S, Thomson, R and Flynn, R (eds) (2004) *Youth in society.* London: Sage.

RSA (2008–11) *Opening minds.* Online. **www.thersa.org/projects/education/opening-minds** (accessed October 2011).

Sanders, J (2011) Derby City Council defend decision to ban homophobic foster couple. Online. **http://news.pinkpaper.com/newsstory/5073/24/3/2011/Derby-City-Council-defend-decision-to-ban-homophobic-foster-couple.aspx** (accessed 9 April 2011).

Shakeshaft, C (1989) *Women in education administration*, 2nd edn. Newbury Park, CA: Sage.

Shakeshaft, C (2006) Gender and educational management in Skelton, C. Francis, B and Smulyan, L (eds) *The Sage Handbook of Gender and Education.* London: Sage.

Sharma, RK (2010) *Issues in teaching learning.* Jaipur: Global Media.

Shepherd, J (2011) Explicit sex education images criticised by Christian group. Online. **www.guardian.co.uk/education/2011/mar/09/sex-education-criticised-christians?INTCMP=ILCNETTXT3487** (accessed 3 November 2011).

Silin, J (2005) Silence, voice and pedagogy, in Yelland, N (ed) *Critical issues in early childhood education.* Maidenhead: Open University Press. p94.

Sinclair Taylor, A (2000) The UN Convention on the Rights of the Child: giving children a voice, in Lewis, A and Lindsay, G (eds) *Researching children's perspectives.* Buckingham: Open University Press. p30.

Spillane, J, Halverson, R and Diamond, J (2001) Investigating school leadership practice: A distributed perspective. *Educational Researcher,* 30(3): 23–28.

Steer, A (2009) *Learning behaviour: Lessons learned – a review of behaviour standards and practices in our schools.* London: Department for Children, Schools and Families. para. 4. 16.

Sternberg, RJ (ed) (1999) *The handbook of creativity.* Cambridge: Cambridge University Press.

Taylor, M and Johnson, R (2002). *School councils. Their role in citizenship and personal and social education.* Slough: National Foundation for Educational Research.

The Muslim Council of Britain (2007) *Towards greater understanding. Meeting the needs of Muslim pupils in state schools. Information and guidance for schools.* London: The Muslim Council of Britain.

Thompson, B (2009) Managing to survive? Issues of gender, management and leadership in initial teacher training. Unpublished PhD thesis, Kings College London.

Tomlinson, S (2005) *Education in a post-welfare society*, 2nd edn. Maidenhead: Open University Press/McGraw–Hill.

UNICEF (2006) *Know your rights and responsibilities.* Online. **www.tagd.org.uk/ Document.ashx?ID=78** (accessed 16 February 2012).

United Nations (1948) The Universal Declaration of Human Rights. Online. **www.un.org/en/documents/udhr/index.shtml** (accessed 11 December 2011).

Waller, T (ed) (2005) *Introduction to early childhood: A multidisciplinary approach.* London: Sage.

Wearing, B (1994) Poor boy, power and gender: The masculinist response to feminism. *Interpretations,* 27(2): 1–21.

Webb, J, Schirato, T and Danaher, G (2002) *Understanding Bourdieu.* London: Sage.

Williams, M (2005) *Leadership for leaders.* London: Thorogood Publishing.

Woolley, R (2008) Communicating effectively, in Cole, M (ed) *Professional attributes and practice.* Abingdon: David Fulton. p94.

Wray, D (1999) *Inquiry in the classroom.* Don Mills, Ontario: Pippin Publishing.

Wyness, M (2006) *Childhood and society: An introduction to the sociology of childhood.* Basingstoke: Palgrave Macmillan.

Index

Added to a page number 't' denotes a table